I0819768

A SEASONING OF LUST

Jane Kohut-Bartels

A Seasoning of Lust
First printed 2008

Available from www.lulu.com

ISBN 978-0-578-01232-2

Printed in the United State of America

CONTENTS

DEDICATION

I am a writer, mostly of erotica. Two years ago I joined ERWA (Erotica Readers and Writers Association) a group of many people, wonderful writers and some who have become friends and writing mentors over the past two years.

I have included in "A Seasoning of Lust" some very short stories (200 words stories or scenes) poetry and a couple of short stories.

It was hard to pick and choose what to put in, and what to leave out. I am sure as soon as I have the printed book in my hand I will groan and say: "How could I have included this piece?"

Well, perhaps it fit the mood du jour, or had a sentimental attachment that escapes me now. There were pieces that didn't make it in this volume. But generally, the works that did, when writing them, spoke to me, either shouted or whispered.

I hope some of them do the same for readers.

There are many people to thank, some were active in the production of this book, many critiqued the works within and gave of their time and talent. Some were just friends and supporters that I met in and out of ERWA. Many outside.

I am also a belly dancer, and I want to thank the gentle training, patience and loving friendship that Aya Arsan and her troupe here in Atlanta has given me since the beginning.

The people I thank are in no order of 'giving'. They all made "A Seasoning of Lust" possible.

Bill Penrose, Nick Nicholson, Rose B. Thorny, Angie Cameron, ERWA, Jerry Steele, Mac the Knife, Ted, 95 year old Aunt Jean in New Jersey, and so many others whose names escape me right now.

A very special thank you to my friend, Bill Penrose who took this manuscript and made it into a book. Also to Bill for his blurb and his encouraging my writing from the very beginning of ERWA. This book wouldn't have existed except for the loving support of these three and many more.

And finally, my son Christopher, who is my techie, and my loving and supportive husband, Fred.

This book is dedicated with love to them.

Jane Kohut-Bartels
Autumn, 2008

JAPANESE INSPIRED VERY SHORT STORIES

A FORTUNATE FATE

Hana Takate was nineteen years old, a courtesan in old Edo. When she appeared in public, men's eyes turned like sunflowers to her sun.

Lovely Hana had bones like melted butter and skin shaped from powder. She was a creature so luminous a flower of purest jade could not compare. When she rose from a nap, wearing a simple gauze robe, free of makeup and perfumes, she floated like a spider's web. A vision of culture and desire, her laugh was a tinkling bell, her hair of *bo* silk, and her movements like cool water.

One day during cherry blossom time, she was entertaining, her robes folded open like gossamer wings, her rouged nipples suckled by another. A young daimyo was admitted to her rooms by mistake. This new lover was so angered he cut off the head of his rival with his long sword in one swift blow.

Hana knelt before him, head down, exposing her swan neck, awaiting death. Seeing her trembling fragility, her obedient meekness, he could not take her life and disappeared to write some bad verse.

She became known as "The Immortal Flower", a courtesan of first rank. She prospered and became fat.

BAD KARMA

Bao Ling sat on the balcony of Floating Wind brothel. A courtesan of low rank, she was deep into writing verse. She now had a scroll of 100 poems, needing revision.

"Bao! Bao! Squat Mother says you are to prepare for honored guest. Come in and apply your cosmetics"

Poor lame Midori was her maid and Bao turned her face obediently to the brushes and powders of her only friend.

"Who is coming?" she said as Midori painted her eyebrows high on her forehead.

"So sorry, but it's Tanaka-san today."

Bao's eyes widened. "Aiiieee! He likes things pushed in odd places!"

"Just do as he wants. We'll have rice balls later."

Tanaka-san's karma was to be short shafted and have peculiar desires. Bao mourned her own karma.

Later as Bao lay under him, he groaned and spread his ass cheeks, signaling Midori to plug his honored hole with an ivory dildo. In her confusion Midori grabbed the slim scroll of poems, plunging it deep. Tanaka-san yelled in delight and flooded the Treasure Grove of Bao with his spunk.

Midori was beaten. Over rice balls, they decided the poems had bad karma and probably belonged where they ended.

THE STILLNESS OF DEATH

Lady Nyo knelt on her cushion, her tea cup before her. She did not move.

Lord Nyo was drunk again and when in his cups, the household scattered for hiding places. In the kitchen was a crawl space. Three servants were hiding their heads under there and a fourth was wearing an iron pot on his head.

Lord Nyo was known for three things: archery, temper and his drunkenness.

Tonight he strung the seven foot bow and donned his quiver high on his back. He looked at the pale face of his wife, his eyes blurry, and remembered the first time he bedded her. She was fifteen. Her body had been powdered silk, bones like butter with the blush of ready passion coursing through her like a tinted stream. She was still beautiful, but too fragile for his tastes. Better a plump courtesan, not all delicate and saddened beauty.

In quick succession he drew back the bow and let five arrows fly through the shoji screen. Each grazed his wives' ear.

Lady Nyo knew her life hung on her stillness. She willed herself dead. Death, after all these years with him, would have been welcome.

Furisode is a kimono worn by unmarried women.

THE GEISHA

The moon floats above the pines, the night cold but dawn finally comes. The Geisha sits on legs grown stiff with waiting, thighs bound in linen. She wears a pink furisode for this occasion but white would be right, the color of mourning, color of death.

Her lover disgraced, he has embraced death, his blood the sacrifice to wipe clean a particular stain. She is to follow, duty fulfilled. Death follows death, a rigid path of hard order, her life mostly of sorrow.

Opening her gown she exposes white skin. The maid, quietly weeping, on her command opens the shoji. Before her a winter landscape, white snow on the rocks, white snow like her skin, soft, melting away. Spring will be soon.

Yes, life mostly of sorrow.

Outside, winter is silent, the snow falling like petals. Ah! She will never see spring or cherry blossoms!

Floating over muted glassine air comes the sound of two monks, Shakuhachi artists, playing flutes to honor the dawn. Such a mournful song, but one that brings rest to her heart.

She smiles, picks up the knife before her and opens her veins. The blood of her line answers for the honor of another.

THE NIGHT OF THE STAIN

Miu stood under the willow, the greenery enveloping her like silk streamers, hiding her. Her maid Zazu was searching for her. These peaceful moments were rare.

"My Lady! I have found the most beautiful gown in the bottom of a chest. It will be perfect for your wedding." Yes, her wedding. Miu parted the willow. Zazu was holding a pale jade silk kimono, embossed with seed pearls and silver embroidery. Miu's breath caught in her throat.

She opened the kimono. There it was, though faded with time. A blood stain.

She remembered when she wore it. He was dead now, but her greatest love.

She closed her eyes and remembered his face, black hair and his perfume. Mixture of sandalwood. She remembered his cock and the ebony dildo he gave her. She remembered the night of that stain, when locked in his powerful arms she screamed out in passion and made the servants scatter outside the shoji. She had bled from the strength of their lovemaking.

Now she was to marry an old man, arranged because of poverty. She would need the dildo. She would marry him in the stained kimono. It wouldn't matter anymore.

THE PUNISHMENT

While binding me for his pleasure, I uttered displeasing words. With a level glance he considered options and too soon decided my punishment.

Grabbing my hair, he pulled me to my feet and opening the shoji screen, forced me into an early spring's snowy morn.

Ordering me to kneel, I obeyed, shivering in fear. Drawing an early cherry blossom from his sleeve (a gift that was to be mine), he threw it at my feet.

It was his pleasure for me to feel the sharpness of the morning until the soft snow covered the flower.

I, who a month ago would not have cared what I said, now trembled with remorse, feeling more than cold air. I knelt in the snow, my bound arms and nakedness revealing my shame. A crow in the cherry tree laughed scornfully.

When love grows deep and the heart overflows, one submits and becomes a slave.

The snow soon covered the blossom at my knees.

He picked me up in his arms, carried me to the brazier and tucked me deep amongst his robes, singing softly of the foolish maiden who would die for the last word.

SEASONAL VERY SHORT STORIES

A REASON FOR THE SEASON

I saw the Cooper's hawk this morning. She landed on the chimney pot outside, probably looking for my miniature hen, Grayson. Four years ago she was a starving fledging who mantled over to me while I fed her cold chicken. She's back this holiday, my spirits lifting. A good Christmas present.

In the middle of the commercialization of Christmas, Nature closes the gap. I have noticed squirrels with pecans in mouths leaping the trees, hawks hunting over now-bare woods, unknown song birds sitting on fences, heard the migration of Sandhill cranes as they honk in formation. You hear their cacophony well before they appear.

There is a brightness to the holly, washed by our early winter rains and the orange of the nandina berries has turned crimson. The smell of woodsmoke in the air and the crispness of mornings mean the earth is going to sleep. We humans should reclaim our past and our fecal plugs and join the slumber party like our brother bears.

Jingle Bells will fade and our tension with it. Looking towards deep winter when the Earth is again silent will restore our balance and calm our nerves with a blanket of peace.

SPRING CAN'T WAIT

Soft mid-winter night where the moon rides the sky like a beggar's cup one-fourth filled. The skeleton trees are silhouetted against the horizon as the light folds into dark velvet.

I think of her loins, tender not rough like the gravel under my feet, but juicy, full and warm, straddling me, her breasts full like the cup of the moon, the shape, not the level.

She spilleth over like the melons of summer.

I come outside and salute the sky, the moon and now the winking stars with a glass of Jura, and see Spring has already taken the land. Winter's hand is still rough on the Earth, but Spring, eternal and forever, bids that Winter move its ass and give room for the birth of the earth. A delicate Couperin melody floats in the chilly wind.

This eternal, whirling dance from season to season, never tiring in its efforts, surprises me with earliest snowbells and the first shy crocus. The red maple is bursting with carmine pompoms on its bare branches, and soon the plum trees will prove as vital.

The earth's gestation is in the air, and life is good.

WINTER WIDOW

At the window she saw the naked trees of winter lit by a slivered crescent moon, casting thin shadows upon frigid ground. Skeletons in the moonlight, ghostly trees, as brittle as her own internal landscape. There was little flesh about her now, she a fresh widow, reduced by grief until resembling the fragile branches outside in the sullen night.

There was a time when she was juicy, ripe with swelling tissue, wet with moisture, velvet of skin. She lapped at life with full lips and embracing gestures. Speared on her husband's cock, she moaned, screamed with laughter and pivoted in sheer joy. Her life had been full, overflowing, desirable, endless, a portrait of promise.

He died one day, and life turned surreal. So much remained, only the reason for living gone. The temperature of life grown colder, like him under the soil.

Outside it started to snow. She watched the gentle coverage of branch, bush and ground, a tender benediction offered to a cradled earth. She went and knelt in the snow, now grateful for this arousal to life and sensation.

She would live, but thought he must be so cold under the snow.

SPRING ORGY

The roses are having an orgy. They haven't the decency to wait for the dark, but ply their lust in the soft, morning light. Randy Graham Thomas is leering. Madame Carriere is blushing. Her pink silk-petaled gown flutters as she twists coyly to avoid his embrace.

By 10:30 the sun warms their scents and foreplay is over. The wind at 11:00 entwines them and pistils and stamens are seriously at it, brushing languorously over parts an hour ago were covered discreetly. At high noon in the heat of the morning, pollen is floating all over the air and even the wide-eyed cats sitting under the tender foilage are blushing.

The garden gnome is licking his lips, while a concrete hand creeps to his crotch.

This fall there will be rosehips aplenty, red nipples packed with tiny seeds, evidence of a springtime lust.

A MISMASH OF VERY SHORT STORIES

THE VALKYRIOR

Helga, Hedwig and Ingrid were summoned to Valhalla. They crossed the rainbow bridge entering Odin's great hall. Two ravens, Hugin and Munin, perched upon his shoulders, as he addressed the warlike virgins.

"My table is lacking the best of warriors. There's a battle brewing below and I command you. Bring back the bravest dead warriors. I would have company and fellowship."

So these three Valkyrior, "Choosers of the slain" rode forth in their strange flickering armor, which flashed over the northern skies, and created the Aurora Borealis.

Ingrid the youngest saw a warrior so beautiful, she would save him. His armor knocked off in battle, she grew lustful. She became an iridescent mist and carried him far from harm. Changing back, she threw herself at his feet, kissing them.

Being a man he grabbed her and took her maidenhood, leaving blood on the earth.

The raven Hugin passing overhead, saw all and croaked into Odin's ear their pleasures.

Odin, thundering anger, ordered them to Valhalla, though the warrior still breathed. Ingrid clung to him, tearful, begging Odin's mercy.

Seeing her devotion, he allowed them life and gave immortality to the warrior. They gave him many grandchildren.

ALI BABA AND HIS FOUR THIEVES

While Ali Baba and his four thieves were drumming last night to wild North African rhythms, I ran to them, giggling, hot and sweaty, fresh from the dance.

Grabbing my dumbek, I wiggled in between two drummers, propped my right foot on a chair and tucked the drum beneath my breast. I tried to catch their rhythms already swirling like looming, stomping ghosts.

They are tolerant, my Berber friends, of the silly belly dancer who would rather drum than dance. They are like my brothers, but that fades when the dumbeks gets serious. Then the primal rhythms heat our blood and strong, dusky hands gallop over the skins.

I am transported to a desert of their making, where they are no longer just waiters in a restaurant, but dangerous blue-skinned veiled men on Arabian steeds and fast camels.

I am thrown over a saddle in front of one.

I see Ali's eyes narrow and Hassim's close, and my nipples harden. The Berbers before me are fierce men, and I am a woman. The drums draw us together in this ancient dance of lust.

I feel sand in my shoes.

GRAHAM THOMAS

She stood quietly in the garden, dappled sunlight falling like a tattered golden veil, crushing a Graham Thomas in her hand. The silky texture slipped through long, bony fingers. A seductive perfume carried upwards, the feel of the petals reminiscent of something she vaguely remembered in the past.

Yes, she remembered now. It was her pussy, soft and puffy, with powdered lips awaiting the frisson of arousal. The man who once kissed those lips was long dead, a pale ghost to her memory.

A tower of rose heads nodded their encouragement. They watched her season after season, the cycle of bush-life matching her own. Grown thin during the years, all gnarled canes beneath and gall, too. Within years both had become feeble. Soon the bush would cover her grave, dropping its petals in remembrance until it, too, faded from earth.

Now Graham Thomas was pleading to cover her mound with his perfumed beauty. He would nestle within the deserted folds of her abandoned sex. He would make her juicy again.

He promised to leave the thorns on the bush.

ILIADIC TALE

(A not so close reading of Homer)

Prince Achilles faced angry King Agamemnon.

"Your Majesty, gettings are keepings with you. Brave men fought gallantly. Your stores and granaries are overflowing. Now you demand I give back my only prize, given by your hand." (*Old Greedyguts!* he thought.)

The maid Briseis *was* desirable. Almond-eyed, slender hipped, golden hair down a tawny back, she was war loot, father a distant king. He wanted her back.

Achilles started to draw his sword, but his divine mother, Thetis appeared as vapor.

"Pretend to give back the maid, and then, my poor child, take revenge. Kill her and spoil Agamemnon's game."

Briseis was led from Achilles quarters to a moored ship. His heart raged, and a quick flash of his sword killed the guards.

"Come fair Briseis, and be my wife." Achilles leaned her back upon a rock and pulled her legs around him. "The first time is unpleasant, but you will grow in desire."

Achilles placed her upon his cock, poor Briseis clung to his neck, and sank slowly down. He plunged into her, and blood covered his sword, Briseis' no longer virginal.

"Come on my cock, Briseis" he muttered, groaning. Briseis did. Twice.
Agamemnon's game was up. Achilles won by spoiling the prize.

ORPHEUS and EURYDICE

Hear my rendering of an oft-told tale, mixed with a leavening of Bullfinch and the sight of Orpheus' lyre in the cosmos.

Orpheus, son of Apollo and Calliope (I can't remember Eurydice's heritage), were to be blessed by Hymen.

He brought no happy omens. His torch smoked and drew tears in all eyes. The flowers wilted and the Gods and Goddesses coughed and sputtered.

Orpheus, master of the lyre, whose notes melted tiger's hearts, made trees uproot and creep near, made rocks soften, loved his Eurydice.

Fate conspires with happiness. Eurydice, chased by shepherd Aristaeus was raped. Now Eurydice's hymen was remade each night for Orpheus' pleasure, and she died a broken, bloody death on the end of Aristaeus' cock.

How fast Orpheus descended to those Stygian depths! His tones pleaded for the return of Eurydice. Sisyphus sat on his rock to listen, Ixion's wheel stood still, and the Furies' eyes were wet with tears. Eurydice came, in her winding shroud, fresh with young death.

Here's the deal. Walk out of Hell and don't look back.

Orpheus! You almost made it! Eurydice, twice dead, disappears.

Sometimes, in both love and death, it only takes one glance.

RANDOM POEMS

O ABSALOM!

O Absalom,
ensnared by your long hair in the
boughs of an oak,
pierced through the heart three times
yet your nature was born only to please.

I, pulled into your mysteries
panting now, yours answer to my heart.
Abandoned by love, given over to lust
charged with stolen rapture
dizzy as a dervish,
one hand upward to Heaven
one hand spilling to Earth
skirts stiffened with sins hard as stone
corrupted over a life time and now
flayed on an unending mandala.

Mystery of Life, unstoppable desire.
O beautiful Absalom, we float upon a divine river
entangled in the reeds of human desire.

This is our nature, this our calling while
flesh answers to flesh.
What quarter be given when the heart is
overwhelmed by passion's excess?

Lie still -- let the waters cleanse our loins
the mud of the banks soothe our wounds,
let our blood mingle with the floating grasses,
our hearts sink beneath the surface.
Let the rivers of Babylon
Carry us away.

THE APPLE TREE

I looked at the apple tree today,
the one the storm did not take,
and saw it still full of apples,
mottled, green/red fruit, some
rotted through with ants gnawing
at the brown-turning flesh
and I thought of the last months
and what was ripening inside you
and we still didn't know….
when your breasts were like
the now ripening apples, globes of heaviness, topped with
brown nipples,
they lay in my cradling hands warm with life and I could
feel them pulse,
the river inside still flowing.

MUSINGS ON A CLOSING DAY

I move my chair
to observe Mt. Fuji-
monstrous perfection
with the cooling crust
of spring snows.

Languid movements
of branches
like a Geisha
unfurling her arm
from a silk kimono
makes petals fall,
 a scented, pink snow that
covers my upturned face
with satin kisses.

Timid winds caress
my limbs,
brings soothing relief
to old and tired bones
brittle now with life's argument
and defeat.

Raked sands of garden
waves are hardly disturbed
by feet like two gray stones.
They continue their flow
around ankles and
I realize again
I am no obstacle to
the proverbial 'sands of time'.

My heart is quieted

by the passage of nothing
for in this nothing
is revealed life's fullness.

THE RIVER

The sun streams in the window,
a jarring benediction
from a loud- mouthed priest.
It falls upon us
as we spoon asleep,
your back turned to me,
my nose on your skin
breathing the miracle of you.

Last night, our first in spent passion,
that particular coin flowed like a river
between us,
you brought hot, wet towels
to clean up the waters left by the flood.

Bending over me,
parting my thighs with your hands,
I wanted you to leave the damp alone,
and slide your hand
into the still wet, faintly pulsing dark chasm,
my hollow jerking and twisting at the end of your cock,

but instead,
I curled up like a fiddle-head fern,
and embraced your dark head with my hands,
pulling your mouth to my own,

and we flowed down that river again.

QUEEN OF SHEBA

She walked right by me, a Queen of Sheba
black skin glinting like steel in the sun,
proud breasts topped with prouder nipples
pointing east to west
her turbaned head hitting the North Star
her jeweled feet the South Pole.
all space between
guarded by curved fangs,
dangerous territory.

Tattooed ribbons flowed down her arms
black snakes with sensuous intent,
the sun shone on gold- tipped teeth
when she parted her dark, stained lips,
rarely a smile, more of a sneer.
Black-kohl eyes flash her disdain,
measuring her vast urban jungle
from the cracked sidewalks littered
with a culture's debris.

I offered her the most honeyed of fruits,
the celestial music of planets,
the jewels of shining, piercing stars
captured in baskets for her fondling,
brought down to earth to surround her with
their unapproachable beauty,
a veil of delight and honor.

Ah! Cruel Queen of Sheba
walked right by me,
no glance in my direction,
she had other fish to fry
though I promised the wealth
and wisdom of Solomon.

TO THE NEW LOVER, #1

Fingers flit over cheeks
rubbed raw during the night
by ardent kisses and the
rough beard of a man in rut.

An early morning's light
peeks through drapes drawn
for modesty's sake
shielding the
sweet debauchery
of the night before.

She feels his hands move to her breasts
and nipples greet their caress,
arising to a new and different
touch, demanding notice.

His dark head moves to kiss her mouth now
dry, her lips bruised with their late passion,
he is filled again with early need and
she feels him push at her thigh.

Eyes barely open, he now knows
the terrain, and with a growl, rolls on top of her,
spreading the sweet apex of her thighs, a hand
in the warm, dark moistness of her sex.

She stretches, remembering the sweet movements
of the night, a savage *pas de deux*, as
an ardent moan escapes from her throat.

This morning, he is gentle, her sex sore,
almost virginal, challenged by the heat

of the night
and with gentle touches, he commands
her arousal,

And calls her out to dance again.

TO THE NEW LOVER, #2

Coming upon him
unexpectantly,
she felt a flutter,
throat-constricting
palms-sweating,
stomach-twisting
lead-in to lust.

He stooped to kiss
both cheeks,
very continental,
old-world charm,
his eyes softening
with new-drawn
affection.

She would rather
he push her against the wall,
pull unsteady legs round his waist
plunge cock into heated cunt
make her scream obscenely
his hips thrusting like no tomorrow,
startle the pedestrians
make the pigeons scatter
and both be arrested
for unseemly public passion.

But instead,
he squeezed her hand,
looked deep into her eyes,
a lingering look that would
feed her fantasies
until they were finally alone.

WINTER WOOD

Walking in the new winter woods
crunch of frozen ground beneath
my boots,
my dog's paws will be sore tonight
for we aim far afield.
I think of this morning when we
argued at breakfast,
the smell of maple bacon should
stop all that, but didn't.

We can't get past the desiccated ghosts
who have taken up residence in our hearts, inviting
slights and outright blows never delivered
but still lingering in the air.

I took the gun loaded with birdshot
in case there was a duck down by the pond.
Were, but they were those sitting ducks
didn't seem right, too easy a target
like this morning at breakfast when either one
of us could have let swing and landed a good one
on tender flesh and raw nerves.

The dog is game for hunting, but my heart
isn't in it.
My thoughts go back to you standing there,
that old apron around your waist,
determined not to let me see tears
and my own cracks and soon I head back with
a peace offering of a bough of holly.

OLSEN'S POND

I returned to the old house,
now still, vacant and
staring with unshaded eyes
upon a snowy front garden,
shrubs overgrown with the
lustiness of summer
now split to the ground
taxed with heavy snow.

I tried to light the parlor woodstove
same cranky cast iron smoker
clanking and rattling
when heated in the best of times
had given up the ghost,
cold metal unyielding to wadded paper
And an old mouse nest.

The silence of the rooms only broken
by hissing wind whipping around the eaves
rattling old bones in the attic
stirring the haunts sleeping in their corners.

It took a time for pine to catch,
the water to turn to coffee.
An old iron skillet served for the bacon
and eggs I brought from the city,
tasting better in the country air.

I looked down at my hands, cracking
in the sharp winter's light,
moisture gone, the air dry,
hair static with electricity,
feet numb from the chill.

I walked down to Olsen's pond
looking through the glassine surface
remembering the boy who had fallen
through the ice while playing hockey
slipping under the thin cover, disappearing
without a sound, noticed when our puck flew
Up in the air and he, the guard, missing.

We skated to the edge, throwing bodies flat
trying to reach him just out of catch,
crying like babies, snot running down our chins,
knowing he was floating just under the ice,
silent like the lamb he was.

Childhood ended then for most of us.
We started to drift away to the city,
our skates and sticks put up, Olsen's
pond deserted like a haunted minefield.

Forty years ago I still remember that day
when I stretched as far as I could
my belly freezing on treacherous ice,
grasping to reach a life just out of sight,
his muffler and stick floating in water,
The boy, the important part,
gone for good from a chilly winter's play.

SEASON'S CHANGE

I took a walk this morning,
The season has changed here
Though where you are they don't.
The dried, brittle grass beneath my feet
Made a consistent crackle,
Echoed by the gossip of sparrows
Above.

The leaves are gone now from the
Birches and maples.
They fell like rain on a fallow ground
One day
And I didn't see them go.

I think of your rounded arms when I see
The shedding birches, the smooth bark like
White skin with a faint pulse of the
River beneath.

Do you remember the river, where it
Scared you to stand close to the bank?
You thought the earth would slip
Inward and
Take you on a wild ride downstream
Where
I couldn't retrieve you,
And I saw for an instant your raised Arms to me, imploring
me silently to
Save you,
Though it never happened and you
Never slipped down the bank and I

Never could save you.

But imagination plays with your mind
When it is all you have left.

SONNETS

EROTICA SEA

O, give me a taste of your cock and tongue
pry open my lips with that soft muscle,
plunge in warm waters of an ocean sung
by lusting mermaids, loins in a tussle,
a clam's foot that tastes the brine of passion
claims undersea caves of another route.

Pull my loins to yours in a riptide grip,
sound my deep warm sea, your cock a stiff mast
the weight of you pushing me downwards fast
hips gyrate in a nautilus spiral.

With your foghorn's groan, semen's saltiness
floods my womb like the moon's tidal offering,
we float weightless, that sweet mystic sea sings,
bodies sway, like abandoned ship's rigging.

LOVE

Stretch me out, both my arms over my head,
The weight of you hard now on my flesh,
Hollow to hollow, hip to hip instead
Tongue entwining tongue, lust so intermeshed,

Legs like twisted branches grown together
Two old trees only thunder from Heaven
Can rattle asunder but our hearts never.
Grafted in lust and love spirits leaven'd

Love is eternal though life be sorrow
Desire burns out of reach, hands not tender
Souls always yearning, day upon morrow
Hearts dance upon glances sometimes render'd

Our lives strain forth with implacable odds,
Love eternal, more the gift of gods.

GRIEF

Her eyes are cast on dreams now unbidden
If her sad glazed eyes, now locked in death's stare
Can pierce memories too broken, hidden
My heart is wretched, no more of life's care.

Past touch of her flesh haunts my fevered brain
The perfume of hair, rounding of soft arms
The swing of her gait, all added to charms
My grief is unbounded, falls like hard rain.

We were so young once, our ardor untried
The touch of her hand upon my sore brow
Soothed all my worries, exhaustion denied
Little is left of my heart, cinder now.

I move through my life, broken and waiting
To join in spirit our final mating.

FATE

Human frailties, wounds that bleed such heated blood
leave a dry vessel without the moisture of love.
the clay reverts to the hollowed and mined ground
cracked with exhausted efforts of all around.

Tears soften venom that pours like a river
knives bring pleasure to hands still covered with love
trembling, can't find the mark, anger aquiver,
plunges into bound flesh, sacrificed like a dove.

A multitude of mourning and cries sound out,
Life's mandala turns without concern or caution
bodies broken, over mankind thin or stout
no one is spared in this universal ocean.

Too soon we give up the hallowed ghost.
To the Father, the Son, or the One who Roasts

LADY NYO POEMS

Lady Nyo is a character in "The Kimono", a novel I am presently writing. She is of 16th century feudal Japan and of a daimyo's court. She writes poetry constantly and talks in verse much to the annoyance of her husband. She is in her late 20's and mostly happily married.

1:

So lonely am I
my soul is like a floating weed
severed at the roots,
drifting aimlessly.

2:

Everyone is asleep.
There is nothing to come between
the moon and my shadow.

3:

From the dream where we made love,
my laughter calls me back
and I search all around me,
my eyes full of tears.

4:

I fell asleep thinking of him

and he came to me.
If I had known it was only a dream
I would never have awakened.

5:

I lean on my elbow
and look at him asleep,
his bosom rising and falling.
It is enough to feed eternity

6:

Clouds sweep the moon.
causing its light to dapple you.
My love! You waver before me
like a ghost under water.

MORE LADY NYO…

A BAD QUARREL

1.

My soul was blossoming
secure in your protective shadow.
I stumbled upon this road we walked
and all was suddenly lost.
The fault perhaps I did not
Tightly grip your hand?

2.

Like a ghost under water
only the moon gives illumination.
Throw a pebble there
and see how fragmented I am.

3.

I can't look in the mirror
when I wake.
(My eyes swollen with last night's grief,
my pillow filled like a lake.)
If I could turn back the hands of the clock,
I would give up those moments of life
to restore lost harmony….

But I dare not look this morning.

4.

It is raining outside,
it is raining within.
Do you think I care about that?
What happened
has disrupted
all the essentials of life.

5.

Who opened the window?
Who let the bees in?
They are the life
I am avoiding.
Their legs have honey on them!
Too sweet for my present mind.

6.

Outside is a tender spring.
Inside it might as well be winter.
There is no warmth
generated by memory.

7.

I am told this is a little death
I will have to bear.
Perhaps I don't want it to end?
Then the thought of living without you,
or the threat of living With you…
would upset my self-pity.

8.

There is nothing from you today.
But then, it was I who moved afar.
I did this from self-hatred,
but found enough to spread around.

9.

When I get to the anger
you will know I am recovering.
Not nicely, there will always be scars
and jagged edges,
tokens of our time together.
Do you feel any of this pain?
No, perhaps not.

10.

My laughter is as hollow
as that stricken tree by the pond.
I have not laughed for a long time.
It strangles in my throat.

11.

This morning I awoke,
and everything was sharp-edged—
my eyes were hardened steel,
my mouth a grim line of dead embers....
but my hands are steady now.

LADY NYO FORGIVES HER HUSBAND

1.

Stop tickling me!
Yes, I forgive you,
but you take such liberties!
Your hands are not clean from
previous crimes.
Go wash them in the snow of
last year's falling.
Then I will reconsider your request.

2.

Look! There is a cardinal,
red as blood and as cocky
as a lord.
See his mate?
She is dull, but has her lipstick
on this morning.

3.

Last night I thought of you.
My face still bears the blushes.
You thought it was good health?
No, just reflects the liberty
of dreams.

4.

(My mind is still shattered
And my heart still sore.)
But I put on a fresh face
full of smiles and polite manner.
It would shock our friends if
they knew the turmoil of
my heart.

5.

You came with a mouthful of 'sorry'
and leave now with other parts eased.
Never mind.
Your coming and going has served a dual purpose.

6.

The spring is so tender.
My heart blooms like the white plums.
Do you think our happiness will last
'til apple time?

7.

Off you go,
and don't look back.
If you turn, you will see serenity.
But behind this mask
is a well of longing.

8.

Last night
I tied my kimono tightly,
bound it with a red silk rope
like an impassioned lover's hands
around a wasp waist,
and kneeling upon a cushion,
awaited the rising of the moon
at the open window.

THE TEMPTATION OF LADY NYO

1.

Yesterday I found a fan with a poem
stuck in my screen.
Today I found another one placed
on my cushion at court.
Do you have a death wish?
Or do you desire the death of me?
You know my husband would kill me.
Would I end my life dishonored?

2.

I see you are as persistent
as the rain in Spring.
Have you no fear?
What is your interest?
Surely I am just another painted face.

3.

I read your poem.
I could do nothing else.
This time it was inked upon
MY fan.

4.

"The wind blows from the north
Chilling my heart.
Only the thought of a touch of your sleeve
Warms me."

Very nice, but my sleeves are not interested.

5.

"I throw acorns
To the darting carp.
With each nut I say a
Prayer for your health."
Lovely sentiment, and I
always grateful for prayers.
But do you think of my reputation
and what you risk?

6.

I see no poetry this morning
though I looked for your usual offering.
I knew your interest was as capricious
as a flight of moths.

THE SHIBARI SERIES

This series was inspired by the rope practice of Mackenzie Cross, a Canadian writer, who introduced me to the concept of shibari.

SHIBARI #1

Japanese hemp coiled about the torso, creating diamonds where there was once only skin, looping back upon itself, over and over. Breasts now defined by a rope cut-out bra, while waist, love handles, now enclosed in more diamonds, thighs entwined. Added turns and thin jute split my cleft with a hard caress, the large knot on the bottom shifting upward. It would tease in mid air.

Dance comes from the earth, through the feet, up and out, giving shape to song. This time I would dance in flight, the pull of ropes challenging gravity, compounding my efforts.

Movements liquid and extreme startled me, the kikkou and hemp anchored me in space, my first taste of freedom in the ropes. Suddenly I felt the sting of a whip and I jerked out of time to the beat. I fell deeper into the dance, determined to continue. Again the whip's sting and I faced a split reality: pain or pleasure. I went inward, deep into the music and rhythm, where movement was birthed and pain banished.

I flew, hollow bird bones filled with joy. Cradled within the ropes I spiraled up from heavy earth.

SHIBARI #2 (THE SPIDER WEB)

Restrained by the hemp to a beam above and to posts at my sides, I was secure in a blue rope karada. It bunched my skin where it bound, creating its own mountains and valleys, distorting my natural figure.

Pain was the door, the portal, the whip applied until I cried "Mercy!" I had slipped into an altered state, far from where pain ate at my flesh. Just back from subspace, I had dangled in the infinite where time stopped and a crude salvation was born.

Looking up at the ropes I was now in a spider web, frozen at all points, the fly caught, splayed in a hemp web 360.

I glanced behind me. The spider was a big one, gently stroking my welts, drinking a glass of water, or perhaps it was green goo. He smiled, now aware I was conscious and with a questioning expression, picked up the single tail and shook it at me.

"More?"

I smiled slyly. Such gluttons we were, the spider and the fly.

SHIBARI #3

Again, I am restrained on all sides, a fly trapped in the stickiness of a dismal fate. I can hear the spider behind me, warming up, flicking the whip, marking his targets on my body, my wings too shredded for further flight.

What am I searching for? I thought salvation, but there was little of that. Perhaps transcendence? At this point, I would settle for any transformation out of here.

The whip caught me by surprise. I jerked forward, lifted six inches in flight with a high scream, the sound pairing pain and confused need. Blackness poured in like oil and I went limp.

I awoke, the burn deep in my feathers. Looking to both sides, my eyes now two sharpened orbs with 6x vision. Hooked beak, my feet wicked talons. A furious shake and I was free of the web, free of the ropes. Extending strong wings, I flew to the top of the beam. With a loud hawk hunting call I surveyed the ground, hungry, need fulfilled - almost.

The spider saw me, only a moment of fear crossed its black eyes before bowing his head to fate.

SHIBARI #4

I flew high but it was spring, and the weak thermals did not support my flight. I was hungry, without food, except for the spider. A freshly fledged hawk must learn how to fend for herself. Beginnings are dangerous.

Cupping my wings, I hovered over a stream, watching the ice break apart far below. Three days of freedom had left me weak, confused and with a troubling need. Breaking my bindings I was now lost, abandoned to nature, cold and alone.

"Hep-Hep-Hep". I heard the 'call-in' of the falconer below me, as I floated over the landscape. Seeing the whirling lure with a rabbit head was too much. Starved, I spiraled downwards, landing with a thump.

"Good Girl" I heard as the man beckoned me to his glove covered with fresh meat. As I mantled over and stepped up, he slipped a jess upon my left leg, another with silver bells on the right.

"Good Girl" I heard again as he tied me tightly to a perch.

"Good Girl" as the hood slipped over my head.

At least no one whips a hawk. And there is always the sky.

SHIBARI #5

For the next week I remained in the mews. During that time I was prodded, examined and weighed. The Falconer was experienced and knew to avoid my feet when I was restrained. I would slice him, even with bindings securing my wings and the hood blinding me.

I was to eat only from his glove. He cooed, watching me as I greedily swallowed down the sparse meal, his dominance enforced.

When I was a woman I yearned for the ropes. I wanted them tightly around my body, 'tender is the bight' so to speak, yet now I pecked, pulled at my leather restraints. One day the Falconer found me hanging upsides down, like a bat, hooded and unhappy, but I gleefully bit him as he righted me on my perch.

Soon after, he put me to the glove and launched me into the air, I screaming in delight.

If I thought I had freedom I was fooled. The Falconer had tethered me with a long hemp rope. He jerked hard and I thumped back to earth.

"Good Girl" I heard through my outrage and humiliation.

"Good Girl" I heard as he pinned me to the ground.

SHIBARI #6
"SUBMISSION"

I remained in the mews for my fall back to earth broke my wing. The cage was large, one I shared with a goshawk only allowed to a Master Falconer.

One day Master claimed me from my perch, set me on his glove and launched me. This time I had no tether and made my escape. Screaming into the wind, I climbed high until he and the hated glove were invisible. I flew with the currents, my eyes bright with freedom.

Suddenly, I was changing, feathers dropping from my breast and wings. I spiraled, awkward in my descent, landing by the same brook once choked with winter's ice. Instead of talons I had a woman's legs and slowly my feathers molted leaving me naked, shivering, my limbs white as the remaining snow peppering the early crocuses. My cry now a sob instead of a hawk's high shriek.

Instinct made me start at the sound of the hunting call and there was the Falconer, a blanket in his hands. He threw both of us down and took his rights, my cooing not of doves. Later, collared in steel with long jesses I walked behind his horse.

SHIBARI #7

The spring was gentle, tender rains like warm tears coursing down on sullen earth. I looked skyward and saw the palest of blue, everything fresh and transparent. Sometimes, when I knew I was not watched, I spread my arms and called out to the wind. My voice was too thin, my bones too solid for flight, chained also with gravity.

One morning I brought meat to the goshawk in the mews. He sidled away refusing my meal. Admiring his powerful wings, thinking of the past, I called to him in chirps as I did when a hawk and he swiveled his head to me. Looking deep into his eye I could see my former freedoms as I passed over mountains and rivers, hunting and soaring, all given up for earthbound comfort.

Freedom and hunger traded for slavery and food.

I knew then what would happen. Captured, I had the power to free. Slipping on my Master's glove, the goshawk stepped up and I worked the belled jesses from both legs.

A launch and he soared over me, screaming his delight. I raised my arms, my spirit in flight, my chains now looser for his freedom.

SHIBARI #8

The Falconer, now my Master, was not a cruel man. I found this out when he realized his goshawk gone. He did not question me as I served him his dinner, nor did he ask anything of me when we slept that night.

Only at morning did I find him watching me with a quizzical look on his face.

"Do you understand the point of keeping a goshawk, girl?"

I shook my head. Rarely did I use my voice in answering him. I did not trust it after so many changes.

"Well, let's say that in freeing him, you have upset the balance of nature."

I looked at him curiously. What balance of nature?

With a slight smile he asked: "What do you intend to cook for dinner tonight?"

Of course! The goshawk hunted and we ate what he killed.

"Know you goshawks are called 'the pot bird'? And since he ate from the glove as you did he will probably starve. That is what I meant by upsetting the balance of nature, girl."

I looked for the goshawk all day until my neck was stiff. My dreams that night were full of broken feathers.

SHIBARI #9

It was weeks of anxiously watching the skies for the goshawk before I gave up. I never saw him again. I learned to trap rabbits and put offal on the roof of the mews in case he flew over.

My Master sometimes watched me from the window, never saying a word about his goshawk. I now set the traps and killed the rabbits and in effect I was the goshawk.

Trapping rabbits is tricky, but soon the spring would bring fiddlehead ferns and tender green dandelions to vary our diet.

One day I passed the mews and there sat a huge bird. I quickly entered, my basket of offal in my arms. He turned his head towards me, and I screamed, the first real sound I made since my capture.

It was a beautiful iridescent bird, having a man's head with a long, red nose. He shook his feathers and crept towards the offal and wrinkled his nose.

"Girl, even a Tengu eats better fare. Get me some meat and saki."

I backed out of the mews, and ran to the house. Transformations be damned, this was a strange one!

SHIBARI #10

(Tengu is a Japanese Demon, with shapeshifting abilities, and usually seen hanging around with Priests and Samurai)

I ran into the house, panting with shock and exertion. A Tengu! Sitting in the mews.

No saki, just my Master's single malt I dare not touch, but found sherry and some cold pieces of rabbit. I wondered if a Tengu, bird/man such as he was, would rather have raw fare. A bird of prey would disdain the cooked rabbit, but he did have a man's face. The leftover rabbit would have to suffice.

My Master was gone, expected at dusk. I walked slowly back to the mews, hoping my mind was playing tricks. There he was, as big as, well, there was the Tengu scowling at my approach.

Human hands appeared from under his hummingbird colored feathers and he greedily grasped the sherry bottle and drank a long gulp.

"Not saki, girl, but good for a thirsty bird." He grinned and his nose got even redder.

"You are thinking, 'why is he here now'? Ah girl, deep cosmic issues. You and me in the mix. One last chance for me to throw off some bad karma."

He finished the sherry, belched and leered at me.

I heard my Master return on his horse.

SHIBARI #11

I ran out of the mews with my offal basket over my arm. I must have looked funny to him because he kicked his horse to hurry to me. Looking down he peered into my eyes and an expression of concern crossed his face.

"What is wrong, girl? You look like you've seen a ghost."

My eyes wandered back to the mews and his followed mine. Dismounting, he let the horse wander into the barn and walked quickly into the mews. I followed him with quick steps.

He pulled on the falconer's glove and approached the Tengu, now looking very much like a large, normal bird. He looked for bands, jesses and bells but found none of course.

"Strange, girl, he would find his way here. Well, perhaps he has promise of hunting if he is young enough to train. I don't know though, he looks rather old to me."

Telling me to draw water and feed him some raw meat, he headed to the house.

The Tengu watched my Master retreat with hawk eyes.

He had a nasty cackle. "Your Master has no idea how old. Feed me well girl, I've got magic to conjure. Scram!"

SHIBARI #12

I came back with the Tengu's dinner that I filched from my own. He wasn't in a pleasant mood when I entered the mews, but certainly ate what I brought him with relish.

"Good". He belched, wiped his mouth with the cloth that covered the basket of food. Leering at me, he winked one eye.

"Sir," I asked, "What am I to call you?" He had started to pick lice from his feathers, crush them and drop them on the ground.

"Sir" will do nicely for now."

"Where did you come from?"

"Ah, the eternal question! Well, I came from Mount Kurama, all Tengu do, but I prefer to haunt Toyko. Like to be a pigeon in a park and look up the skirts of the women there. Nothing more, just like to see muffs and thighs, favorite parts."

I was a bit taken back. I read something of Tengu. "Don't you hang with Buddhist priests?"

He barked a short laugh. "Picked on the wrong one. Powerful Yamabushi. Bad karma
now. That's why I'm here. You need me."

He wasn't the pleasantest of Tengu, but he certainly was the first. Perhaps need went both ways.

SHIBARI #13

The spring warmed up and Tengu and I took walks through the countryside. He adopted the guise of a large, golden eagle in case my Master saw us walking in the fields above the house.

The soft air nuzzled my arms and legs and the Tengu shook out his wings, opening and closing his large beak, drinking in the sweet air.

I told him of my past, the strange transformations from woman to bug to hawk and back to woman. His eyes got big with surprise.

"You have one fucked up karma, girl. And I thought mine was shitty."

My Master had placed me in light chains, and I caught the Tengu contemplating them.

"Ah", he said, reading my mind, "I'm wondering if they will interfere with your wings." I was afraid to ask anything, but my heart started to race.

Later that morning, he twisted my chains into a tighter bondage. He now used my soft body for ikebana, fertile soil for him to place the stems of spring flowers and twigs in my hollows, fill my lap and hair with long grasses, giving new meaning to gardening and beauty and gentleness.

The end so far...

POETRY

HAIKU

Cold rain sweeps the streets
Even ducks seek shelter now
Feathers drop in haste

A man carries wood
Dinner now to be prepared
A hen clucks her last.

The glance at a wrist
White, the pulse of a river
Tiny beat of life

A woman in bed
Kimono revealing breast
Snow on Mt. Fuji

Snow falls on meadows
Crows pick at last harvest seeds
Spring now far away

Swirling winds of fall
Make kimonos lift to knees
Modesty is lost

Cherry red toenails
Peek out from the warm blanket.
Deep snow cools ardor.

Willows whip about
Her kimono flares open
Eyes savor plump thighs.

White makeup drips
The hard heat and mosquitos
Make maiko languid.

Girls chase falling leaves
Plump thighs give delight to eyes
Mothers do not smile.

Hard wind from the north
Chills both man and animal.
Life is not certain.

A swirl of blossoms
Caught in the water's current
Begins the season.

Sorrow floats like air
Strong winds blow throughout the night
Plague of death descends.

Coming near the flame
I was burned by sharp brightness
My dullness consumed.

This is the problem!
Do not give over your soul
It returns tattered.

A modest woman
Does not seek comfort with thieves
Emptiness is fate.

Human frailties
Wounds that bleed such heated blood
A dry vessel left.

Tears soften venom
Knives bring satisfaction to
Hands still covered with love.

No heart is exempt
Distance makes no barrier
The sun rises, sets.

The heart is brittle
Hands can not soothe its aching
Only honest words.

A woman in grief
A force that races nature
Better now anger.

Minute to the hour
The heart races on the edge
Sharpened existence.

Birds fly in blue sky
All is grey upon the earth
Heart is stopped with bile.

A woman in heat
Lover's delay makes her burn
Strong force of nature.

The pale flame flickers
Hooded lust enters the room
Restrained, she trembles.

Trickle of warm blood
Courses slowly down her breast,
The pain yet unfelt.

Low, uttered whisper
"Mercy". There is none within
There is none outside.

Transcendence achieved
But at what price was it bought?
Only time will tell.

A spider grasps prey
Weaving knots of shibari
Suspends with delight!

TANKAS

The moon floats on wisps
Of clouds that extend outward
Tendrils of white fire
Burned up in the universe
Gauzy ghosts of nothingness.

Shooting star crosses
Upended bowl of blue night
Imagination
Fires up with excited gaze
A moment-- and all is gone.

The heart is brittle.
Hands can not soothe its aching
only honest words
can make the sore mind attend
unless pain ever constant.

This is the problem!
Do not give over your soul,
it returns tattered.
What tailor can mend the rips?
The fabric too frayed by life.

A modest woman
does not seek comfort with thieves
Emptiness is fate.
Better her eyes turn upwards
to Heaven, soul comforted.

Human frailties
wounds that bleed such heated blood
leave a dry vessel.
Without the moisture of love
the clay reverts to the ground.

Tears soften venom.
Knives bring satisfaction to
hands still covered with love.
Trembling, can't find the mark
but the shame returns, pierces.

The heart is brittle.
Hands can not soothe its aching
only honest words
can make the sore mind attend
unless pain ever constant.

A woman in grief,
is force that races nature.
Better now anger
contempt will replace her love.
She will be stronger for it.

Minute to the hour
The heart races on the edge,
sharpened existence.
Feet trammel the rocky ground
While pain flies up to Heaven.

Birds fly in the blue.
All is gray upon the earth,
heart is stopped with bile.
White crane lifts off lake water,
my heart tries to follow it.

Shall an old gray wolf
subdue a woman like me?
I shall be born soon.
The wolf head I will cut off
and nail the pelt to the cross.

The morning wren sings,
I stand in the moonlit dawn
kimono wrapped tight.
Last night I made my peace
now free from all attachments.

Bolts of lightening flash!
The sky brightens like the day
too soon it darkens.
My eyes opened or closed see
the futility of love.

Had I not known life
I would have thought it all dreams.
Who is to tell truth?
It comes at too sharp a price.
Better to bear flattery.

SHORT STORIES

MLLE DUCHAMPS

Many years ago, there was an elderly gentleman who lived along with his invalid daughter Marie, in the Vercors region of France, near the Swiss Alps. Comte d'Epinay was impoverished, due to the death of so many relatives by Madame Guillotine, and the taxation upon those of the aristocracy who managed to keep their heads.

For a while, Comte d'Epinay was addressed as "Citizen d'Epinay", but the country folk reverted to M d'Epinay, and an uneasy peace existed. M d'Epinay lived without the luxuries of his youth in a decaying house, too small to be considered a chateau and too large for economy. The roofs leaked, the fireplaces could benefit from a good cleaning, but beyond a shotgun blast up the chimneys every few years, there was little improvement in the draw. The tiles tumbled off the roofs with the Mistral, which swept down the Alps and did much damage. It was locally held that anyone who went mad with the sounds of the wind would be pardoned of their crimes.

The household staff had dwindled to a housekeeper and a steward, M and Mme Pennay, leftovers from the *ancien régime* along with Mme Fournard, who was the governess for Marie d'Epiney. Social visits had diminished in the early years after the Terror, even this far removed from Paris. Gone were the parties and fetes of M d'Epinay's early marriage, and gone was his wife. She had grown feeble with each packet of news from the capitol, and finally one morning, was found stiff and cold in her bed. It was said Madame had died of grief for her beloved France. The locals thought otherwise, but as isolated people do, they believed evil had blown down from the mountains and played a hand in all misfortunes in the countryside.

This part of France was prey to all kinds of superstition and haunts. If a cow stopped giving her rich milk and gave a watery stream, it was the hand of a witch. If a flock of chickens started eating their eggs, it was because a malevolent spirit haunted a farmer's house.

The spring came early and with it the rains. Each day, Marie d'Epinay would limp her way around the bedroom, and holding onto the chairs and sofa, she would make her way slowly to the big window that gave her the outside world. Mlle d'Epinay's governess had grown to be a companion, for her charge was now in her twenties. Mme Fournard was herself almost elderly, a woman whose life had passed her by in the service of the d'Epinay child.

"Marie!"

Mme Fournard had come into the room and saw her charge leaning on the windowsill, staring out at the pouring rain. "Come away from the window, *ma chérie*. The cold from this rain will make you sick."

Marie's usual thought passed across her mind when Mme started her scolding. "How much sicker will I become before death takes me away?" But this of course she did not impart to her governess. Mme Fournard was deeply religious, or superstitious, and to Marie's thinking, there was little difference. Perhaps it was the loneliness of her days spent in dank rooms with a book in hand that created such cynicism in Mlle.

One late afternoon, in a heavy downpour, there was a long knocking at the door. The housekeeper, grumbling at the impatience of the knocker, hurried to answer. A man was standing there on the steps with water running off his hat, and in his arms a bundle. Without a word, the man entered. The housekeeper, of course, would not deny him entrance in such weather.

"Thank you, Madame. We have been traveling from the east and our carriage has overturned on the road. Mlle Duchamp has been injured and your house was the only one I could see in this rain. Please forgive the intrusion."

The knocking drew the household, M d'Epinay amongst them. "Mme Fournard, please help Mme Pennay, take this young woman to a bed." M d'Epinay was a gracious soul. His own lack of fortune would never turn his heart cold to the distressed.

When Mlle Duchamp was deposited in a bed, and the man had withdrawn to the warm kitchen, Mme Fournard opened the blanket and saw an almost lifeless young woman. She had drab red hair, made worse by the rain, such pale skin that there was no bloom of life, and a breast that barely rose. Stripping her garments, the two women noticed she had strange markings, almost like lashes, that crisscrossed her body. She appeared to be in her twenties, but she could have been older or younger. It was impossible to tell due to her present condition.

Over the course of a few days Mlle Duchamp regained consciousness but remained very weak regardless good broth and simples applied to her lips. The man who had brought her went out in the pouring rain and was never seen again. No trace of a carriage was found later on the road, for M. d'Epinay sent men out to help put things to right.

Mlle d'Epinay heard from her governess of the guest in the next bedroom. She was curious to see the girl. She had a key to the adjoining bedroom, and when Mme Fournard was down in the kitchen or somewhere in the house, she would unlock the door between the rooms and would make her way slowly into the bedroom, lurching from chair to table, and finally to the bedside. Usually the woman was asleep, muttering in a deep dream. Today she was awake but motionless.

"You are finally awake! *Bon*! I am Marie d'Epinay, this is my father's house. I am glad to see that you have recovered yourself."

The young woman before her struggled to focus her eyes and a small smile formed on her lips.

"I am so cold, Mlle. I am so cold. Come to me and keep me warm."

Marie did not see any reason to refuse this poor woman, and went down beside her, over the top of the blankets. She gingerly put her arms around the woman and felt the bones of her shoulders. Louise Duchamp, for that was her Christian name, sighed sweetly, and the two of them fell into sleep. They awoke later that afternoon, both refreshed and talking and this is how Mme Fournard found them, when she came with a tray for Mlle Duchamp.

It was true the house was cold and damp, and remained that way until the heat of the summer, so Mme Fournard did not have any immediate objection to the two young women taking a nap together. She had a servant stoke up the fire and propped upon pillows, both women would read aloud to each other, and both sets of cheeks seemed to color with some health.

Marie would sleep in her own room during the night, but insisted Mme Fournard leave the adjoining door open so she could hear the sighs of her now dear Louise.

One night Marie awoke in the darkness and gasped in fright. It was only Louise standing there over her, as if sleepwalking. Pulling back the covers Marie beckoned for Louise to join her, for the spring was a long and wet one and the rooms still damp. Louise lay down on her pillow, wrapping her arms around Marie. She drew her close, and kissed her shoulder, travelling with little kisses down the virginal breast of Marie. At first Marie stiffened in her arms, then relaxed, for surely Louise was dreaming and could not know what she was doing. Louise found a soft nipple through Marie's nightgown and started to suckle her. Marie, surprised, felt a tremor travel from her breast down her body. She gave a little moan and Louise smiled, stopped and fell back asleep.

After that, Louise would visit Marie and when the stillness of the house was complete and nothing disturbed the absolute silence except the moaning of the wind outside, she would fasten her lips upon Marie's breast. She would suck and nibble, and Marie would moan. When Marie awoke in the morning, Louise was asleep in her own bed, the roses in her cheeks showing her recovery. Marie remembered nothing unusual, except a strange, continuing dream that left her languid far into the morning.

The visits continued for several weeks. One night, Marie found Louise beside her, and this time, Louise had bunched up the muslin of her nightgown. Slowly, almost like a moth's gentle touch, Marie felt her fingers in her sex. She stroked back and forth, back and forth, barely touching the flesh. But for Marie, it felt like an angel's wing to her, and she experienced a sensation that had her hips arch off the mattress.

The next night, Marie found Louise in her bed again, and this time she moved her head lower and lower, until she was blowing her sweet breath on Marie. Marie, trapped in this sensation for which she had no rational name, spread her legs slightly. Louise parted Marie's nether lips and with her tongue, lapped and tickled, sucked and swirled until Marie started to scream. A hand shot up from between Marie's thighs and clamped over her mouth. This was no impediment to the new sensation, for the joy she felt unleashed deep in her body, soared out her throat and into that hand. Kissing it, crying with sweet relief, Marie fell asleep and in the morning Louise was back in her own bed.

After that, Louise brought another game to their night time hours. Pain. At first she would bite a little of Marie's lips, and then when Marie jumped, she would apply her lips and tongue to the part of Marie that flew her to heaven. Each night, Louise would increase the pain just a little, and Marie looked forward to the pain because in her mind it became mixed with the extreme pleasure Louise imparted. More and more pain, and then the resulting pleasure. Marie's lips became bloody and tender, but that a small sacrifice for the ecstasy she felt. Their play touched Louise too, for her pale and sallow skin had more bloom, obviously due to the great devotion she had for Marie.

One night Marie and Louise were playing their love game. Marie's pleasure was so intense she had to stuff a pillow over her mouth when she was thrown into ecstasy. Louise now was sitting on her thighs, with Marie's parts pulled up to her mouth, sucking and biting and lapping and swallowing the juices that poured from Marie. It quite overcame Marie, and she went limp with spent passion.

That morning a carriage appeared at the door. Louise Duchamp was downstairs tying her bonnet. She was smiling at herself in the large glass in the hall. She looked radiant, her red hair curled and bright, her complexion glowing, her green eyes gleaming with secrets. A restored beauty and Mme Fournard quite amazed with the young woman she was watching at the bottom of the stairs. She hadn't thought Mlle Duchamp would recover, much less to such an extent!

"Oh, Madame, you should check on Mlle d'Epinay. I thought her a bit restless during the night, but when I looked, she was fine. Perhaps a nightmare?"

Mme Fournard agreed and climbed the stairs. Soon a loud scream erupted from upstairs, followed by a piteous moan. At the same instant, Mlle Duchamp blew a kiss at her reflection, walked out the front door and was helped into the carriage.

Marie d'Epinay was dead, pale as a ghost in her bed, and Louise Duchamp was never again seen in the Vercors region of France.

The End

THE DEVIL IN PARIS

Madame Gormosy is a Devil. She can change her sex at will, from Louise Gormosy to Louis Gormosy. John Garret is also a Devil, but not so powerful. They have known each other for centuries as devils generally do. The scene is Paris, in the 1770's.

Madame Louise Gormosy stood by the tall window, looking down at the rain-slicked street. Paris was cold and dreary this spring. Wood had gone up in price, and a timely delivery was a matter of bribes. That would be the concern of her steward, but he had disappeared. Already her servants were breaking up small cabinets and chairs to burn in the main salon and kitchen. She could hear the smashing of wood somewhere in the large apartment.

Madame shivered for the room was chilly. She was used to a higher heat. *Ah,* she thought, *if ever I see him again, I will make him pay with his life for my discomfort. I will tear his stomach open with my nails and cook his liver.*

She had a visitor, a sullen-looking Englishman now with his large frame stretched across her sofa. John Garrett had been a friend for many years. He was an easy-going devil and good company when in the proper temper. She looked at him with a sideways glance, a smile forming on her painted lips. Patting her high-dressed hair and smoothing the gray satin front of her gown, she wondered what had put him in such a mood. She remembered he was quite a wit when not bothered with serious thought. She hoped he would reform his manners, for she wanted nothing to spoil the afternoon. The rain could not be helped.

"John Garrett!" Madame's natural voice was low pitched but now showed her exasperation. "Are you going to continue your gloom and attempt to sour my day?"

Garrett, his eyes drawn slowly from the low burning flames of a fire that barely reached outside the hearth, looked up at her. He stared for a long minute, a sneer forming on his handsome face.

"We are alone," Garrett said quietly. "I know you better as "Louis". Why this behavior between two old friends?"

Madame did not answer him. She walked to the double door, locked it and threw the key into his lap. For a moment she stood there, with her head cocked to the side, an elegant older women, dressed in the latest fashion, and only a sharp rise in the middle of her skirt gave warning of what was to happen.

In an instant, "Louise Gormosy" was "Louis Gormosy". Gone was Madame's satin overdress, the high coifed and perfumed hair. A bit of the makeup remained, but it was the fashion amongst Parisian men. Louis laughed at the expression on Garrett's face. He now was a slight-figured man, above middle age, with powdered hair and white silk stockings, like any other Parisian gentlemen of current fashion.

John Garrett knew his friend was not just any *man* in Paris. He was a demon, an important one, the Archduke Demon of Lust, with sixty legions under his command.

Louis Gormosy had ridden out of Hell on a white camel and tormented the earth. It could not be helped; it was his nature to do so.

Ah, he thought, I miss my camel… along with my legions, but tant pis! Paris' cobblestones were hard on her aging hooves.* He was a powerful denizen of Hell, and with status, came responsibilities.

His guest, John Garrett, was also a demon, but not of the same stature. Louis Gormosy was not sure of Garrett's actual position in Hell, but knew him to have the patronage of the powerful Archduke Abigor, close to the throne. With friends like that, even the powerful Demon of Lust had to watch his hoof. The thought of Abigor's name sent shivers down Gormosy's ossified spine. Hell was a place of no forgiveness, and even a cinder rolled by accident under the foot of another would throw into motion an endless vendetta. There was no accounting for the spitefulness of devils. It was mother's milk to them.

Louis Gormosy chuckled at his guest's surprised expression seeing his transformation.

"Oh come, John, surely you are getting used to my little trick? *Non?* Well then, I have another reason to invite you here, beside the parlor trick. This evening I am expecting some guests, and I have a particular reason for you to meet them."

John Garrett sat up, stretching his legs. "Are you planning a little entertainment this evening? You know, Louis, one never can tell with you." His expressive face registered his suspicion.

Louis Gormosy lay a finger aside his nose and winked. "You have come at a good time, John. I expect a young woman, a girl actually. She is the daughter of a neighbor in the country. She is about eighteen and her mother is anxious to have her married."

"I am almost afraid to ask, Louis. What part do you play?"

John Garrett looked at his friend from half-closed lids, like a cat settling in for a long story.

Monsieur Gormosy walked to the window and looked out at the still pouring rain. He turned his head slightly and gave Garrett a nervous smile before peering down at the street, watching for a carriage to stop at his door.

"Madame Luciern is a silly woman, a bit more stupid than usual. She has a daughter on her hands she complains is a 'bookworm'. Ah! *Bon Dieu*! So the young woman will educate herself with novels and newsprint. *Tant pis*!"

Louis Gormosy threw up his hands in disgust. The words "Good God" had a strange sound in his mouth, just shy of a gurgle.

"You still don't tell me what your part is in this affair."

Gormosy turned and looked at his friend. "Better you ask me what *your* part is."

John Garrett sucked his breath in sharply, and let out with a soft, "Oh no, Louis!"

Louis gestured with his hands outward, all Gallic charm, and continued his appeal. "What is a little fun amongst devils, neh? You have certain…ah…attributes that I unfortunately, do not have."

"The starch issue again, Louis?" Garrett's words rattled Louis and he winced.

"*Quel dommage*! I don't know if this is a little trick of Heaven or Hell, John, but it persists. I begin the attack, a few thrusts with the sword, and even with one parry, I wilt."

And, thought Louis sadly, *it always came down to what devil had more 'reach'. It always came down to a measurement. Here on earth the length of the cock, and in Hell, the amount of control.*

For a brief moment, he consoled himself with a quick fantasy, of hiding in the draperies, watching Garrett hunched over Mlle, spread eagle on the bed, whimpering in terror, awaiting with no rescue the huge and purple member John possessed. Louis had seen the weapon before, in another century perhaps. He was surprised to realize that this thought created a twitch in his own.

Was it the defilement of Mlle or the masculine appearance of Garrett that created this twitch? No matter, devils did not distinguish between such issues. It was all of a piece.

And about this little sprinkling of starch? Miracles of miracles… there was hope yet!

"So, what is your plan and why should I care?"

Monsieur bit on the side of his thumb, thinking how to present his case.

"I have not seen the young woman. Her mother keeps her well hidden in the house. If she is a bookworm as the mother says, perhaps any attempt here in Paris to marry her off will be impossible. Perhaps she is ugly!"

"Or perhaps she has no bosom," said Garrett from his sofa, eyes wandering back to the fire.

"Or perhaps she has a harelip!" said Gormosy. "What do I know? I have not seen the poor girl."

With a grimace, Gormosy shook out his hand. He had bitten deeply into his flesh, and blood spurted from his thumb.

Garrett asked, "Does she have a good fortune?"

"*Non*, unfortunately not. Madame Luciern is a widow and her estate is lessened with the behavior of her oldest son. That young man has no sense at cards...and worse luck! I would give him some pointers in faro, but I do not cheat at cards."

What a big lie, thought Louis, laughing to himself. There was honor amongst devils but not at cards. What was the worse that could happen? A duel, you die, you come back fresh and new, with another chance to cheat life. And at cards.

"But!" continued Louis, raising a finger into the air for dramatic emphasis. "She has an honorable name! That is worth something, I think."

"Hah," said Garrett. "Perhaps of worth to mortals. But it *is* something."

The blood continued to spurt from Gormosy's thumb. "*Merde*". He pulled a sooty linen handkerchief from his pocket and wrapped up his thumb.

"So, what do you intend to do with Mademoiselle?" Garrett queried, "Do you have a cuckold in mind?"

"Why would he be a cuckold, *mon ami*? I have all intention of marrying her to someone worthy and with a good fortune."

"And if she is not marriageable due to this harelip or flat bosom? What do you intend then for Mademoiselle?" asked Garrett.

"I intend to make her a whore."

There. It was out, thought Gormosy. Let him chew on that. There was profit to be made here, and he, Louis, would take the advantage.

"Why do you need me?" John Garrett's eyes half closed again as he looked at his friend who was grinning broadly.

"If I can not obtain an acceptable offer, I will need your - ah, efforts, John."

"Meaning? Come Louis, do not make me beat it out of you."

"You will seduce her. You will make her more pliable for her gentleman callers…I, of course, will revert back to Madame, for this is all her mother knows of me, and you will play…"

"Hold on, Louis. Do you or don't you intend to get her a husband?"

"How should I know?" Louis Gormosy gave a shrug of his shoulders and presented his palms upward.

"I don't know if she has a harelip or an unfortunate bosom," he said. " We both, my old friend, will find out this evening."

* * *

John Garrett stood at the window looking out at the rain when he heard the knock on the door. He watched Louis cross his hands over his breast and shake his head violently. Louis became Louise again. *Voila*! Her high coifed powdered hair, the satin dress, the tight corset and breasts returned. As many times as he witnessed this transformation, it always took him by surprise. Louis was one tricky devil. A snap of Louis' fingers and the door unlocked.

Garrett watched Madame and Mlle. Luciern entered the room, Madame like a clipper ship in full rig. Madame was a short, plump woman, middle- aged, with powdered hair that showed the effects of the rain. Her dark plum, satin gown was ten years out of fashion. She wore little face powder and there were honest wrinkles and age-spots enough to signify that Madame was no longer young. Kissing Louise on both cheeks she shook herself, rather like a hen ruffling her feathers. Louise gestured for her to sit.

Garrett listened to Madame Luciern introduce her daughter to her hostess. Louise took the young woman's hands in hers, studying her carefully and called for him to come be introduced.

Garrett bowed over Madame Luciern's hand and watched her face color with delight. Mlle Luciern had no such reaction to his presence. Her face remained expressionless.

Taking a chair across from Mlle, he listened to Louise Gormosy ask the mother questions about their trip from the countryside. The two older women were soon lost in chatter and he had a chance to observe the silent young woman.

His first impression of Mlle was favorable. She was slender, with an underdeveloped bosom, a fine complexion and a pretty mouth. She *did* look like a bookworm, he thought with a chuckle. She had a serious demeanor, with pale gray eyes and dark brows that did not arch in the necessary fashion. Fine brown hair pulled into a simple unadorned bun exposed a slender neck. He was curious. He had his fill of coquettes and fashionable young women in Paris. They were of a general order, all schooled in manners to attract a man's attention and hold it captive for an afternoon. Their charms passed through him like water. How bored he had become with the women of Paris!

In Mlle Luciern he saw something different. Something intriguing and virginal, but virginity had little value in Paris. He laughed to himself. Virtue was good for children but pointless in an attractive woman. Already the gloom of his mood was lifting in the presence of a rather mysterious young woman.

The two Madames were lost in conversation and twittering with laughter as old friends do. Both her mother and Louise seemingly forgot Mlle. Her face was politely blank, trained to assume a mask in company, but Garrett could see she was not empty of thought. Her fine eyes narrowed as she listened to her mother and Louise rattle on and a pained look cracked the mask.

"You have been in Paris before?" Garrett's voice was low enough to not disturb the chatter of the two older women. Mlle Luciern turned her gray eyes to his and answered his question quietly, with little interest reflected in her voice.

"*Oui*, Monsieur, I have visited Paris before, but not recently. I was a girl when I was last here." Her voice was almost husky, and the pitch of it surprised him. Most young women were taught to have 'musical' voices in company, to laugh as affectedly as a tinkling bell. Mlle Luciern seemed unspoiled by such manners.

He did not have a chance to question her further, for the sound of Mlle's voice made her mother remember her.

"M. Garrett", said Madame with a bright smile. "Margot-Elisabeth was a little girl the last time we were here, only about twelve. She is now nineteen years of age, and a stay with Madame Gormosy will bring some color to her cheeks and some polish to her manners. Ah, Bon Dieu! The countryside is good for virtue but there is little opportunity were we live to make her a wife!"

Mlle Luciern's face showed distress at her mother's words. Garrett saw how Madame Gormosy's eyes glittered.

"Ah, my dear Marie," Gormosy said to the mother. "We will polish the apple and find her a mate. She has promise, but is too pale in the face. Perhaps a bit of rouge and the labors of my hairdresser?"

Madame Luciern laughed out loud at Gormosy's words. "Bon chance, Louise! I can barely get Margot-Elisabeth to brush her hair!"

Poor Mlle Luciern blushed at her mother's words and Garrett suppressed a smile. Margot meant 'pearl' and this one would need quite a bit of polish to catch a husband in Paris.

Garrett tried to make small conversation with Mlle but she was now as shy as unpolished. The two older women chatted away without stopping for breath and the conversation was all about Margot-Elisabeth, unconcerned with her growing discomfort.

Garrett heard the amount of funds pledged by Madame Luciern to Gormosy, and almost whistled aloud. A dressmaker would be sent for immediately.

"Ah, Louise," said Madame Luciern with a look of gratitude. "You work your magic with Margot-Elisabeth. In your competent hands I am sure she will bloom."

Garrett wondered how much 'magic' would be needed by Louise, and how her mother would react *if* she knew the source of Madame's....ah, magic.

How droll it was. Mother Luciern to leave her precious daughter in the hands of a devil. All the rosaries in France would not amount to a hill of shit once Louise got her claws into the prey.

Garrett laughed to himself. Tant pis! The bargain was struck. The Devil would have his due.

* * *

A week later, John Garrett was shown into Madame's apartment by an old servant. He glanced at the dark and wizened man and smelled brimstone. Madame was known to choose her servants carefully. Life could be a subterranean maze in Paris. He knew other demons in the city and all were not friendly devils.

"Ah, John! Bonjour!" Madame was drinking tea with a young woman, one Garrett did not immediately recognize.

"You remember Mlle. Luciern? What changes we have wrought! Such an elegant young woman. What man in his right mind could resist her! Could you, John?"

Ah, thought Garrett. Madame is up to her old tricks. She insists in making me part of her plan for this young woman.

Madame's eyes glittered as she turned to look at the young woman sitting across the tea table. Garrett bowed over the proffered hand of Louise, and then stood back to look at Mlle. Luciern.

Madame had indeed worked her magic. Mlle. was coifed and gowned like a young, elegant Parisian matron. He admired her hair, piled high on her head, with many curls and loops and one long curled tendril- like, a thick sausage over her shoulder. At least Madame's hairdresser had forgone the powder and her natural color was preserved. Mlle's complexion was good but now she had some bloom in her cheeks. He knew this was all art, for Louise was an expert with faces and makeup. He saw Mlle. had only two black satin patches on her face, one near the left eye, and one near the mouth, to draw attention to her painted lips. They did look alluring to him. They looked like they were stung by an amorous bee.

Garrett cocked his head to the side and let his gaze travel down her figure. Her morning dress was light blue silk. Ruffles framed her breast. Garrett let his eyes linger only a second, but Mlle. did present a lovely bosom to onlookers. He knew this was due to more of Madame's magic – this time with pads in the corset. Round, delicate mounds above and the merest of rouged nipples appeared like little mouse noses peeking over the tops of the corset. Such was the fashion for seduction. He wondered how far Madame had corrupted her student.

"No, Madame Gormosy, no man could resist such a beautiful young woman."

Garrett was surprised to see Margot blush so deeply. At least Madame's instructions had not destroyed this vestige of virtue in the girl.

"Mlle. is an good student, John. She learns fast and takes an interest in her future. Her mother will be proud of her. We will get her matched up with the proper husband soon enough. But as I have told Mlle. Margot, there is plenty time for an engagement. Now is to be given to sharpening her feminine skills. That way she will attract the best prospect for her future happiness. *Mais bon Dieu*! She is still so young and innocent. We must hone her wit and deportment. Nothing like the polish upon an apple to attract the proper bites."

Garrett stared at Madame Gormosy. He could easily see through her designs, but of course, the young woman was too naïve to understand what was happening right under her nose. She *was* a pretty morsel, and it was hard to take his eyes from parts of her. The swell of her breast, how gently they rose with an almost imperceptible movement. He could feast his eyes on those two tender pieces of flesh all morning. How much more alluring they would be if she were panting, he thought. A sly smile appeared on his face.

Ah, Madame Gormosy was full of devilry this morning.

Louise Gormosy spoke with a tone of excitement. "Today we will work on the great science of "coquetry". *Non,* M.

Garrett, do not laugh, for women have their own science. Let the men work with fire and chemicals. We women have our own fire and it is called "Les Passions!"

Garrett winced and hoped Mlle. Margot would forgive the bad prose of her patroness. But Madame would press her case.

"Surely Mlle. Margot has higher aspirations than to be a housewife to her husband. It is a most contemptible and unfashionable position for any women of breeding, and has no social standing except for a parson's wife or a lowly farmer's. *Ah Dieu*! Mlle. is made by nature for much finer things!"

Garrett wondered if the word "God" did not burn the inside of Madame's mouth, but since she was an old devil, he imagined she would have a mouth immune to heat. Still, he had heard this speech before, but he could not remember when. Perhaps it was another time in another century, while attending Madame under similar circumstances, that she had used these same words. They seemed familiar to him in any case. He heard her drone on.

"Now, Mlle. Margot, advice today is seen as ridiculous to be given, and even more ridiculous to be taken, but your dear *maman* would want you to listen to me very closely. *Alors*! She has given you into my hands for more than to fluff your beautiful hair and plump your fine bosom. It is her choicest desire to prepare you for entrance into the best of society and this is the path to catch the eyes of a husband. Have you read Madame d'Effine's letters? *Non*? Pity. But I can supply you a copy of her book. Or better yet, I can give you the benefit of my long experience."

Garrett could not stop a smile creeping across his face. Mlle Margot would have no idea just how long that experience really was. Yes, Mlle Luciern, it goes back a long way. Whether Madame could read his mind, which was standard fare amongst devils, or she caught a glimpse of his sly smile, she turned around suddenly and gave Garrett a jaundiced look. His face went neutral and he closed his eyes in compliance. He would not interrupt her behavior. Besides, it was an entertaining for a morning's visit.

"Now, Mlle.Margot. Virtue is all very fine and good, but to get a husband, or any admirer, a woman must use what attributes she has and more. A fine voice, the ability to cut to the heart of a man's desire just with the cast of your eyes, the flutter of your fan, ah! There is so much to learn, but we will persist. Now, M.Garrett, please attend to Mlle. and lead her around the room, *s'il vous plait*.

Garrett stood and offered his arm to Mlle. Margot. They walked around the large salon, Mlle. Margot only standing as high as his chest. He was a tall and well-built man, with broad shoulders, and Mlle. petite next to him. He observed her blush as she placed her hand on his and looked up into his face.

Entertaining as Madame was, he was beginning to have his doubts about her plans. He believed this young woman to be innocent. He rarely, now that he thought of it, came across a woman so - uncorrupted, and certainly not in Paris. The thought crossed his mind: *Quelle dommage*, as Madame liked to say. Perhaps he would have his own plan for Mlle. Luciern. What was a little competition between devils? They had shared tender morsels before in their long history.

"*Eh bien*! *Ecoutez moi*! John, give me the advantage of your eyes. Tell me what you think are the best points of Mlle.'s figure. Does that style of dress, the color suit her the best, *mon ami*? Speak out loud what her beau would say, and let us see how Mlle. reacts to such praise!"

Ah, it was clear what Madame's plan was now! Madame was a terrible devil this morning, and she would have her fun at the expense of the painful blushes of Mlle. He decided to turn the game to his own advantage, and perhaps spare Mlle some pain. She, or course, could not 'see' his thoughts.

John Garrett cocked his head to one side, as if to appraise the young woman before him, but his mind raced with such pleasant thoughts. Scenes of Mlle with her skirts flipped up over her waist, her legs spread open and his purple cock posed at the door of her altar. Her tears spurting from her eyes like translucent pearls, as he contemplated the spurt from his cock, and the rush of Heaven he would soon savor as his cold member plunged into the warmth of her cunt.

Ah, her tears and screams of terror as he ripped through her maidenhood would only make his delight in this rape complete! It was a while since he had himself such a tasty morsel and he would enjoy it fully. His own cock started to twitch with his thoughts and he had to suppress a broad smile.

At that very moment, the old devil servant of Madame Gormosy slipped into the room and approaching quickly, whispered into the ear of his mistress. Madame cocked her head towards his mouth, and though she did not take her eyes from John Garrett and Mlle. Luciern, Garrett saw they grew dark with concern. Muttering some curses low under her breath, she rose and went with her servant from the room, forgetting her two guests.

Garrett took the time of Madame's absence to lead Mlle. Luciern to a chair and to sit down across from her. He observed Mlle. sink gratefully into her seat, and with a motion beneath her skirts, kick off one shoe.

"Ah, Mlle, does your foot hurt?"

"M.Garrett, I can not get used to these narrow shoes Madame makes me wear. I am not used to this fashion. And if you would know further, I am not used to these headaches. They are from my hair pulled from my head and pinned so tightly. And I can breathe only a little. Madame demands my corset be laced tight." Mlle. blushed, but Garrett could hear in the distress in her voice.

"Ah! I sympathize. Perhaps you think what Madame does here is far off the mark?"

"I don't understand what you mean, Monsieur." Another sharp kick under her skirts and off came the other shoe.

"Mlle Luciern. Forgive my blunt words, but Madame is an "old fogey" as we say in England. She means well, but she is generations behind in her thinking."

How many generations Mlle could never guess.

Tears formed in Mlle. Luciern's eyes, and she shook her head. Garrett could only sympathize.

"Here, Mlle. Let me do something for your comfort. I will take all the blame, but tant pis! I am an old friend of Madame's and used to her ways."

He stood and moved behind Mlle's chair. With practiced movements, he removed the pins from her hair and spread them from their high peaks and down her back. With gentle hands he massaged her temples and she groaned in relief.

"Ah! *Bon Dieu,* Monsieur. That feels so good. My poor head was about to explode. Madame means well, but she does not seem to suffer pain like the rest of us. I saw her put on a hat the other day and plunge a pin into her head. *Mon Dieu*! She said she did not hit her skin but her hair, but to me, ah goodness! To my eyes, it seemed to go through her head!"

Garrett smiled from behind Mlle's chair. In fact, he had seen Madame do this before and other such things and had warned her if observed her game would be over. Madame had laughed, she had been doing such tricks for centuries. Besides, the winds of Paris were strong and her hat would blow off if she didn't get a good layer of skin beneath her long pin.

"Madame has a thick skull, Mlle. Luciern", Garrett said with a droll tone. " She is used to all sorts of torture for fashion."

Garrett looked down Mlle. Luciern's bosom and watch the gentle curves rise and fall with her breathing. Too bad his plans for Mlle. did not include a seduction. He would like to savor those two young mounds in his mouth. But it would be a passing fancy and his plans for Mlle. Luciern's future did not include this fleeting pleasure. He had a more lasting pleasure to savor.

And his good friend Louis would be the poorer for it.

* * *

John Garrett was standing behind Mlle. kneading her temples when Madame Gormosy entered the room.

"Ah!-- Oh no! What have you done to Mlle's hair, John? All the work and effort of my hairdresser! Ah well, it can't be helped now. Would you like me to leave?"

Madame's voice cut into the silence and Mlle. Luciern jumped from her chair. She had almost fallen asleep, Garrett's hands soothing her nerves. But she was young and obeyed orders, her face showing her distress.

"Oh Madame! Forgive me! My head was pounding and I thought I would be sick with the headache. Monsieur Garrett has saved me from my pain. Please, I beg you, I am very sorry about the hair."

Madame cocked her head at Garrett and raised her eyebrows. He just smiled and closed his eyes like an owl. He did this many times with Madame. It was his way of signaling he would not answer her questions. He could be as stubborn as Madame was persistent.

"Well, Mlle.," she said with a sniff, "if you are recovered, perhaps we can salvage this morning with a lesson." She would put aside her annoyance and continued with Mlle's instruction, but gave Garrett a withering glance first.

"Perhaps we can start with 'The Art of Seduction'. Do not laugh M. Garrett! Do not *dare* laugh. These are important lessons I impart to Mlle. Her future happiness rests upon honing what she has been given naturally. We must polish the apple some more until she can attract the fruitful nibbles."

Garrett almost groaned aloud. Louis was stuck in this apple cart.

Madame sat down across from Mlle. who had hurriedly twisted her hair into a chignon.

"Attendez-moi! Seduction by a man is his act of attaining the affections of a woman, of becoming deeply enamoured, and applauding her for her generosity and attention."

Garrett moved to the window where he could look out at the street below and listen to Madame. When he heard her definition of seduction, he almost guffawed. Ah, Madame, he thought. You *meant* to say that the great art of seduction is that of gaining a woman's affections under pretence of being enamoured, when you really despise the woman for her vanity and weakness in playing your game. But of course, your pigeon will know no better.

Again, whether there was an unseen current between thoughts, or Garrett actually *did* laugh at Madame's words, she whipped her head around to look at him, her mouth tight against her teeth.

"Ah, Mlle.," Madame continued. "Seduction is a little game between a man and a woman which leads to great results. Do not be discouraged by what the moralists think or say. Seduction is the engine that drives *amours*. *Amour* leads to marriage and to happiness in the future."

Mlle. Luciern nodded her head, seeming to attend carefully to what Madame was saying. She appeared to be a diligent student.

"Now, consider the fan. A woman can make a great conversation of love with just the flick of a fan. *Regardez-moi.*"

Garrett watched as Madame picked up a white silk fan from a little table by her chair and opened it, holding it just beneath her eyes. Isolated by the fan's whiteness, her eyes glittered like diamonds. Mlle. Luciern's own eyes widened at the effect.

"When you put the fan's handle to your lips, you are saying "Kiss me." When you twirl the fan in the left hand, you signal: "We are being watched." Fan held over the left ear means: "I wish to get rid of you. Allez!" Fanning yourself slowly, ever so slowly means, "I am married." Fanning quickly, "I am engaged." Hiding the eyes behind a fully opened fan, like so, means "I love you." Now, Mlle., you show me what you have learned from my efforts."

Mlle. Luciern took the fan from Madame's hand and did as she was told. She hesitated on a number of turns, but Garrett thought that was to be expected.

"*Eh bien*! Now, we will extend the lesson. With the flick of the fan like so—" Madame started another lesson of the fan, when she noticed large tears collecting in the eyes of Mlle. Luciern. Suddenly Mlle. burst out crying and threw herself dramatically onto the floor, clutching the skirts of Madame Gormosy.

"What in Hell's name—" Madame forgot her manners and looked with surprise at the young woman now sobbing into the fabric of Madame's dress.

"Oh, Madame Gormosy, I can no longer deceive you! I am already engaged, though my maman does not know of this. She suspects something but she would die a thousand deaths if she knew all!"

Madame Gormosy stood up suddenly and moved from the clutches of the young woman as she would at a grabbing beggar. She looked down at her, a cold sneer on her face.

"Ah. So, my time and efforts are to be wasted on you? Well, who is he, this great beau of yours? Is he a groom? Your maman's steward? Who, girl, out with it. Do not defy me!"

Mlle. Luciern stayed on her knees, her face streaming with her tears, her hands clasped in supplication before her.

"Madame, my maman did not deceive you. It was I who deceived you. My dear maman thought it was over for I steeled my heart and hid my emotions behind my books. I was determined to give him up, my Etain, but it is too late. I am expecting a child!"

Madame's breath sounded like a rasp in her throat and her face appeared blackened with rage.

"You little devil! You little whore! You come here, instill yourself into my tender affections and you have deceived me! Where is your honor? Where is your breeding? You are no better than a gutterslut! You mother will know what you are, why am I wasting words upon you? Out of my house, you whore, you little—"

Madame raised her hand and was about to descend with it across the face of the stricken, pale Mlle. Luciern, when Garrett crossed the room at the first words of Madame. He had seen her temper before and knew what she was. He grabbed Madame's hand and held it firmly so she could not strike the young woman. Madame whirled around, her face distorted with her anger and she hissed like a snake. At that very moment, she did appear like a viper, with her cold, glittery eyes. Suddenly her tongue flipped out of her mouth, a forked tongue like a snake! He had seen many tricks of Madame before, but this was a new one. Later, when he had time to reflect, he realized that it was not a trick, but very much a part of the nature of Madame. After all, he thought, the serpent figured in the story of Lust, and Madame Gormosy was, after all, the Demon of Lust.

Whether because of her passion or her tight corset, Mlle. Luciern's eyes rolled back into her head and she fainted away. It was a mercy. Mlle. would not witness what happened next.

John Garrett kept a hard grip upon Madame's arm, raised up in the air, and Madame continued to hiss at him. He knew devils could use more or less magic against each other, and Garrett played a waiting game with her. But he knew enough to put distance between them, and dropping her arm, stepped behind a sofa with utmost haste.

"You have lost, Louise, she is of no benefit to you now. Let the girl go with your blessing. Play the generous Madame and let her return to her mother and her fate."

"You!" Madame's voice came back to her. She no longer hissed like a snake. But Garrett observed there was no cessation in her rage.

"You would stay my arm? You, not even a proper Devil? The Archduke Abigor only knows what you are, yet you counter my behavior to this little slut? Do you know what I can do to you? I could turn you to cinders right now along with your friend!"

"But you won't dare, Louise, because of what Abigor will do to you. Do you want to try his humor? Do you want to find out what Abigor will do to you and all you know? Is this little woman before you, now senseless, worth the risk you take? And, knowing Abigor's affection for me, you know what fate you will have. There will be no fire of Hell hot enough to punish you. Abigor will cook up his own punishment. Don't chance it, Louise. Think about your beloved camel."

Garrett knew Louise Gormosy on a better day might have thought of her camel, but today she was in an inconsolable rage. She couldn't stand that Fate had frustrated all her fun.

It just wasn't fair.

But Madame Gormosy could not contain her anger, for it was consuming her before Garrett's eyes. Her face began to darken, and she began to stamp her foot hard on the floor. Within seconds she was jumping up and down, and suddenly she was on fire! Before Garrett could move, she was nothing more than a cinder herself, and black ash floated down to the floor, to collect in a puddle of soot.

Tant pis, thought Garrett. She will be back. She always came back.

A fortnight later.....

Garrett heard gossip Mlle. Luciern was sent home to her mother with a considerable fortune. He heard from impeccable sources this was to appease the mother but also to allow Mlle and her beloved to start life together.

The money went a long way to sooth Madame Luciern's passions over circumstances, but what could she do? Etain d'Aubringe did not have a fortune, but he did have an old name, and with the money given by the generous Madame Gormosy, Madame Luciern had her satisfaction. Her daughter was married, supplied with a fortune and Madame had the prospects of a grandson.

* * *

That spring, a strange sight was seen in the fashionable boulevards of Paris. A woman, heavily veiled, with a golden girdle surrounding her waist and a crescent moon headdress, was seen leaving Paris on a large camel. Behind her walked her household, a collection of dark-skinned little men and women, who left sooty hoof prints behind them on the cobblestones. Paris had never seen such a parade, and this one passed in utter silence.

Except for the camel. She complained loudly with groans and spat upon all she could reach. But those who saw her-- the camel, not the veiled rider-- would long remember the intelligence that gleamed from those eyes.

The End.

LA VENDETTA

Glossary for this story:

Viva il Coltello! (Long live the knife!) Yelled at the performance of castrati singing from the audience (a good thing)
Teste di fantasia: fantasy heads
Fregna: vagina, or in some parts slang for pussy
Bagascia: bitch
Sronzo di merda: fucking bastard....a curse thrown indiscriminately
Coglinno: Balls! A rather joyful, exuberant expression.
Per carita! : for pity's sake!
Che cazzo!: What the fuck!
Paigioni (Prison in Venice: The Leads (under the roof...for the worst prisoners...or the Wells, dank and cold. Either way, unless you are Casanova, you generally don't escape.)
Ponte dei Sospiri: Bridge of Sighs
Cornuto: culkold, horns....
Ciscebo: male companion, an escort.
Puttana- whore

Maria de Guiseppa Agnesi Faini sprawled in a brocade-covered chair. The day was hot. Venice was generally hot, humid and moldy. She crinkled her nose at the smell of the water and slime eating the rotting stucco sides of the villa.

Her apartments were on the third floor but there was still very little air this sultry morning. She could hear the gondola men singing their usual songs of coy, beautiful women and brokenhearted lovers as they plied their way down the Grand Canal. They sang of local courtesans, their songs advertising their attributes, much as the sellers of fish or fruit sang of their ware's desirability. "A lira for a breast, with a couple of oranges to sweeten the deal!"

Signora Faini squirmed in her chair. The brocade was hot to her skin, though she wore a muslin morning dress. Sweat dripped down the viola curve of her back to the crease of her buttocks and she scratched where it tickled. L'Inglese had introduced muslin and it was all the rage in Venice this season. She thought them a bloodless race and a country of bad teeth.

'Where is he?' She tapped her foot impatiently. *'He better bring some good gossip for his lateness.'*

Signor Alessandro Balsamo was her friend. Actually he was her *ciscebo*, tolerated by her husband because Signor Balsamo was a *castrato*. He had been cut when only a young boy (*"Viva il coltello!"* the audience yelled when he appeared on the stage) and sang until his voice disappeared. Other patrons supported him, but alas, Signor Balsamo was growing old and unattractive. His nose was arching to meet his chin, his belly could no longer be contained in his waistcoat and even his corset was now uncomfortable.

Signora Faini sighed. This heat would not let up, and there were at least two more months to bear. She promenaded upon the stones of San Marco plaza until she had worn out 20 pairs of slippers in one month. Now her feet hurt.

She thought of her new lover and her nipples hardened. Her hand strayed to her bosom and she squeezed a breast, rubbing shapely thighs together. A soft groan escaped her throat.

He was an officer, a dashing lieutenant, now on maneuvers somewhere across the Alps. She remembered the first time, when in Signora Mortanti's garden, with her skirts flipped over his kneeling form before her and his lips on her swollen little nut. She caught the eye of her husband and had the presence of mind to flutter her fan at him. He barely acknowledged her so intent was he in arguing the latest political scandal. She inched her way around the tree she was leaning upon to better obscure their behavior. Her lover obediently followed on his knees, never missing a lick. There would have been two scandals discussed that soft, spring night, and this one ending in bloodshed.

Ah, she missed her Alfredo! He was bold, but perhaps all Romans were so. Venice was a wicked city, and there were plenty of places to indulge in passionate embraces. Her husband's gondola was a cozy place, with the canopy making them snug if a bit too warm inside. A few extra lira to their boatman, and she was assured of her secrets. Of course, they could never be completely unclothed, but the necessary parts *'d'amour'* were available. They tried numerous positions, but the best for her was to bounce upon his cock. Then the boatman did not have to compensate for the side to side thrusts of her lover. Her hands found her mound, the dark curly hair that spread over her secret place, not so secret anymore to Alfredo. She dipped a small, plump hand into the gathering wetness. *'Ah, Alfredo! I miss your long cock.'* Not the insignificant dagger of her husband. No, a real sword, one that pierced to her empty womb and she could take in her mouth like a regular *puttana*. The weight of his balls in her hands were like the golden------

"Signora?" A maid knocked upon her door, stopping her thoughts.

"Signor Balsamo has arrived."

"Well, let him in." Signora Faini's tone expressed her annoyance at the stupid maid.

Signor Balsamo entered and made his best leg. His wig was freshly curled and his waistcoat beautifully embroidered. He was a small, stout man, and still there was a certain charm about him.

Signora barely nodded her head. She continued to fan herself with her limp lace handkerchief, the very one she had used to wipe her hand upon.

"So, Allesandro, my love, you dare to show up late...again?"

"Forgive me, my dearest Maria, there was a large puppet show at San Marco. I thought of you and your love of puppets and perhaps we could walk down and see. They are quite remarkable, almost life sized. The staging is well done."

Ah, thought Signora Faini. Puppets! I am in the mood for such entertainment. I won't have to wear out another pair of slippers. I must remind myself to either hide the shoemaker's bill or start lying to my husband. He will start yelling again, and there goes my fun.'

The signora rang a small porcelain hand bell and called for her personal maid.

Signor Balsamo did not remove himself, for he had been present many times when she was at her toilette. He had little interest in a woman's charms, with an exception. He sat, leaning his chin on his cane and watched her being undressed by her maid.

She shed the morning dress, a confection of muslin and ruffles. Then, stepping out of two petticoats, she stood in a chemise. Already corseted, the maid went behind the

Signora and tightened her laces. Sitting, she lifted a slim leg to her maid, not caring that she exposed her *fregna* to the eyes of her *ciscebo*. He blinked, knowing she did it to humiliate him. It was an old and cruel game she played.

Today, she was even crueler. Lifting both breasts from her corset, she examined the nipples. She knew her *ciscebo* had an attachment to women's breasts, probably something from his childhood. She twisted each nipple, making the small dark pink flesh stand at attention. Her eyes narrowed as she stared at the Signor. She knew he wanted a suck, something she rarely rewarded him with. She could see the hunger, his mouth open like a fish and his eyes droopy with a sadness as he sat, his chin propped on the head of his cane. She found a perverse thrill in hurting him. He was such a child, so malleable, so predictable.

Rolling up each silk stocking, the maid tied garters around the Signora's knees. Then she hurried to a large armoire. Opening it, she awaited her mistress' decision.

"No, not anything heavy this morning, it grows too hot and already the morning breezes are gone. Perhaps a silk. What do you think, Alessandro? Perhaps this watered blue with the ecru lace? Does it look cool to you?"

Signor Balsamo had been present for this game many times. If he said 'yes' to her selection, she would discard it. If he said "no" she would consider it, but there would be layers of clothes spread on the floor and sofas before Signora made up her mind. She was woman! What could one expect?

Sitting at the vanity while completing her toilette, she suffered her maid to pin her hair high on her head. Dark, chestnut curls tumbled to her shoulders. At least they would not create heat on the back of her neck. She was a small woman, like a china doll, all curves and bright eyes and rose tinted lips. She rose and turned to her *ciscebo*.

"Ah, Signora! A vision of radiant beauty, a cornucopia of delights, a ----"

"Enough, Allessandro. You weary me with the same chants. Let us leave, though the hour not fashionable. Come Alessandro, you have promised me a puppet show and perhaps a *glace*?

"Ah, something sweet would be very nice! The ice from the Alps is packed in straw. Last time I got a bit of chaff in my ice, this time I will run the vendor through with my sword."

Signora Faini laughed, her tones like a tinkling bell. "Ah, Alessandro, you are *such* a man, so bold and advancing. Too bad about the missing parts."

With that she grabbed up her parasol and took his arm, not caring for the hurt in his eyes. He was to pay, and pay dearly for making her wait this morning.

* * *

The sunlight was bright but there were huge, puffy clouds floating across the deep blue sky. The water reflected the light like a million, million diamonds thrown on the surface by a very rich Prince. Carefully being handed into her gondola by Signor Balsamo, the Signora settled her dress around her, and raised her parasol. Signor Balsamo sat next to her, rocking the gondola as he stepped in. They floated down the Grand Canal, Signor Balsamo watching her nod at a few other gondolas, some friends, more enemies. She made many of them as he found out over the two years of their acquaintance. Regardless, a public courtesy would have to be maintained. "Keep your friends close and your enemies closer" was Signor Faini's personal motto. It had much meaning lately. He might be a *cornuto,* but he was a wise *cornuto,* thought Signor Balsamo.

They crossed under the Ponte dei Sospiri and past the Paigioni, docked and entered San. Marco palazzo. A million pigeons took flight, to circle the plaza and return in great circling spirals to the same stones. The iridescence of their feathers were like tiny winged prisms, caught by the sun. The Palazzo Ducale occupied one side of San Marco's, with its white confection of marble, Moorish tracery. Signora Faini walked beside Signor Balsamo, her arm entwined in his. He swung his cane with the forward movement of his right leg, and swished it to make the vendors and beggars scatter from their path.

The palazzo was crowded today, even as the bells sounded and the cannon fired, declaring the hour. The sounds of musicians and the bray of vendors added to the festivities. There, before them, rose up a stage, with a good crowd fronting the entertainment in already in progress.

It was a very large boxed stage, with a black curtain stretching across the wooden frame where the puppets performed. A roof peaked up behind it. Signora Faini recognized 'Punchinello' a hunchbacked character with a beak of a nose, and clapped her hands in glee.

Signor Balsamo laughed, and infected with her happiness, said, "Ah! Punchinello! Coglinni! Does he never change, my dear? He is universal for bravery, for laziness, for pride and bawdiness! He embodies the best and worst in mankind. Bravo, my friend!"

Signor Balsamo greeted this huge headed, almost human sized puppet with the enthusiasm one would greet an old friend. Perhaps he was related.

"Ah! He is ugly, and that never changes!" An observation from someone in the crowd created laughter.

The *teste di fantasia* in Venice were known in Europe to be the finest. But this was not a Venetian production, but the work of a Russian, who was known as a Count, or perhaps he was a Prince. Who could tell? The mystery surrounding M. Swartzskya was thick as the fog over the canals in winter.

They watched the puppets and marveled how realistic they seemed. Dressed in sumptuous fashion, even if a few years out of date, their puppetry revealed only by the wires that went from their moving parts to high above where the puppeteer was controlling them, they were almost human to observers.

A dance, an awkward embrace, the tangling of wires, the sound of puppet feet hitting the stage and on occasion, a groan. Ah, this Count Swartzskya was a genius! The Doge himself would be entertained, for Signora Faini and Signor Balsamo had never seen such a display of pure delight! All the gold in Venice couldn't replace the sheer magic of Swartzskya!

The sound of a chamber orchestra floated over the palazzo and Signor Balsamo sighed.

"Ah, Maria, they are playing il Prete Rosso's music. Ah! I never heard him, but my sainted father did. What a wonderful violinist the Red Priest, he said. Quick as lightening on the strings, and the heartstrings too, my little dove! So many Signoras opened their corsets and gave him their hearts and love and other small pieces of their devotion. He was quite the scandal in his youth. And a priest!"

"But you know, Alessandro, every priest has a mistress. How could all these *puttani* exist without the Church?" Signora sniffed in contempt, twirling her silk parasol above her head.

The sounds of Vivaldi's music wafted through the air, adding to the spectacle before them. Suddenly, as if the puppets could hear the music, as if they had become animated with human sentiment and had blood coursing through papier mache veins, they bowed and did a stately minuet. How gracefully did the unseen puppeteer lift the wires binding limbs and life. How perfectly did wooden, painted puppets, faces frozen in carved sentiment, with eyes strangely human, flashing with passion, express such intelligence!

Signora Faini was overcome, and a few silly tears gathered in her eyes. Ah, Madonna!

The combination of the music and the display before her was hitting a hole in her soul, pulling at her own heartstrings. Signor Balsamo patted her hand, a strange smile upon his own countenance.

"Would you like to meet Count Swartzskya? I have had the privilege, Maria, and you will not forget the man easily. This I assure you."

Before she had a chance to agree, a loud rumble of thunder drowned out the music and all eyes looked upward. With curses from the men and screams and laughter from the women, it started to pour down on all standing in the palazzo. The rain was relentless and they could hear *'Stronzo di merda!'*, *'Per carita!'* and *'Che cazzo!'* from the musicians as they scrambled to protect their delicate instruments.

Signora Faini's parasol, meant for the sun was soaked. Signor Balsamo drew his arm around her small waist and guided them behind the stage. There was a door and a man, who looked Signor Balsamo in the eye and bowed them in.

Maria looked around at the structure. It was big, almost as big as the reception room in her villa, but the ceiling not as high. There were crates on the sides of the painted, wooden walls, chairs and a large table cluttered with puppetry crossbars, carpentry tools, clothes, all directly behind the stage. As she shook her parasol, the water spun off in clear rainbows of light, landing on the carpeted floor.

Suddenly, from the back of the stage, a huge man appeared as if out of the smoke of a large fire. Maria's eyes widened as she watched the man come silently towards them. Her breath caught in her throat and her heart pounded.

"Ah, Count Swartzskya! Thank you for receiving us. The sudden rain...."
Signor Balsamo's words faded away and he shrugged his shoulders, his eyes locked on the man who stood looming over them.

"May I present Signora Faini, Sir? Signora is the lady I was mentioning before. She has a passion for puppets, Count."

The Count took the hand of Signora Faini and kissed it, she unmoving, her eyes fixed on his face.

Count Swartzskya stood before Maria and she thought, *'I wouldn't come up to his chest! What a remarkably formed creature.'*

Maria had reason for amazement. The Count, perhaps in his late forties, was
well over six feet tall. He had black hair, shot with grey and worn in a pigtail at his neck. The fact that he wore no wig would have been remarkable enough in Venice. That he was so large a man was even more striking. He would stand head and shoulders over any crowd in Venice. His hands were huge and long fingered, his thighs were bulging with muscles. Obviously he had either been a horseman or a soldier. Everything about him reeked of a physical power. Signora Faini seemed quite overwhelmed by his presence, as her eyes impolitely fanned over his face.

Overhead she could hear the crackle of lightening and the boom of horrendous thunder. She shivered and jumped each time the windows of the room reflected the raging storm outside. Suddenly she screamed, for the lightening struck close and the hair rose on her arms. She jumped right into the arms of Count Swartzskya and stayed there, trembling like a leaf.

"Oh, Madame! Do not concern yourself with what is happening outside in Zeus' court. You are safe with me. Come, have tea and settle yourself."

Count Swartzskaya's voice was a deep as the thunder, but soothing.

He led them from the main room to a little chamber, where a servant set a table for tea. Signora Faini appeared grateful for the hot cup of tea. She was shivering.

As she drank one cup and then another, the two men talked and her eyes started to close. It seemed she could barely hold her head up.

Balsamo and the Count continued their discourse in low voices, ignoring Signora Faini sitting at the tea table.

"She has it coming, *la bagascia*, but no permanent damage, agreed?"

"But of course, it will just be something frivolous, a small humiliation."

"But will she remember it?"

"No, she will have no memory of this day at all. However, I can arrange for that to change. What is your pleasure, Signor?"

"No, no, our original plan will be enough – this time, Count."

Swartzskya tossed a bag of coin to Signor Balsamo and he hoisted it in his palm. A broad smile creased his face, as he addressed Signora Faini, now sprawled in her chair, one slipper off her delicate foot.

"Maria, my dear girl, sometimes you go too far in your wickedness. But you will pay the piper later tonight…or shall I say…the Count?"

With those final words he laughed and left, whistling a piece of his beloved Vivaldi.

* * *

Signora Faini could hear Balsamo but could not respond. It was as if she was made of wood, like the puppets before the rain drove her into the shelter of Count Swartzskya and into his arms. Madonna! Everything felt wooden, numb about her and her breath barely moved her bosom. She could hear but she could not speak or move her limbs. She was like a puppet awaiting the wires to animate her body.

The Count leaned over and his finger made a trail from throat to cleavage, his eyes staring intently, his face close enough to kiss her. She could not avoid him and suddenly she felt his fleshy lips as he bit her mouth, drawing a little blood. She could only register fear with her eyes.

The Count busied himself with a little squeeze here, a sharp pinch there, and Maria could not feel his hands molesting her. She could only follow his behavior with a limited movement of her eyes.

"You know, Maria, his Holiness and you share a common desire. He loves puppets too, just like you. But he will never have the privilege of being one."

Signora Faini could hear him but could not respond.

"Ah, sweet Maria, some paint to fix your pretty little face, a costume, some wires and you will be ready for a performance. Tonight you will dance before the Doge and his guests. Wonder if they will recognize you? Ah, no matter, I will make you disappear to them in case any are guests of his Holiness. It is a subtle but sharp little revenge of your good friend Signor Balsamo, no? He will be sitting there, enjoying your puppet antics and your memory of this night will be his alone."

The Count stood and stretched, throwing out his arms over his head. It would be a long night and he had much work. He regarded the little doll of a woman before him, still sitting in her chair, silent, only her eyes animated, and chuckled.

"Ah, Maria…some women learn lessons easily, and some take a bit of the twisting of the wires to get their attention. Perhaps after tonight you will think again before you scorn your Signor Balsamo for his missing parts?"

"Come, Maria, drink a bit more tea. It will fortify you. Is it too bitter? Here, let me add just a little more 'special sugar'. It will do the trick."

The Count obligingly held the delicate porcelain teacup to her rosy lips and filled her mouth with tea. She sputtered, but swallowed, her eyes filling with tears.

Maria couldn't protest, she had no voice. Only the terror in her eyes registered she was even alive.

"Ah, look Maria! Your eyes are sparkling! Tonight you will be the belladonna of the stage. Of course, tomorrow the critics will say your acting was a bit 'wooden' but what do they know?"

The End

www.ingramcontent.com/pod-product-compliance
Lightning Source LLC
LaVergne TN
LVHW091009080826
845145LV00003B/1190

* 9 7 8 0 5 7 8 0 1 2 3 2 2 *